Praise for *On Thinking Institutionally*

"*On Thinking Institutionally* is in the best tradition of Tocqueville—an updated critique of the individualism that has been America's strength and its weakness. Hugh Heclo focuses attention upon an aspect of modernity that has been too long neglected: the failure of our institutions—social, political, religious, economic—to elicit any sense of loyalty, and thus the volatility and frailty of society itself."

—Gertrude Himmelfarb, Distinguished Professor Emeritus,
City University of New York

"In a world that has become pathologically anti-institutional, Hugh Heclo's book *On Thinking Institutionally* will be welcomed and savored by everyone who yearns to reconnect with the moral purposes with which institutions make meaning for those who persist in navigating between the universal and the particular, between what is given and what is not yet fulfilled. Whether experiencing institutions as president of General Motors, or as a religious congregant, as a member of a family, or as a tenured professor convinced that his or her university administration has lost its way, Heclo offers not a shallow self-help book, but the prospect of recovering a way of being in the world that, though uphill all the way, promises a sense of inner integrity that makes the journey worthwhile. This is not a book for a narrow segment of readers, but for anyone dealing seriously with the human predicament, or seeking passion and renewal for the rest of the journey with institutions."

—James R. Wilburn, Dean,
Pepperdine University School of Public Policy

"In *On Thinking Institutionally,* one of the country's preeminent political scientists offers important reflections on morally responsible governance and on the forces—economic, political, and cultural—that make good governance so challenging in our time. Heclo reminds us that political 'office' must not be separated from its original meaning of 'duty,' and that institutions provide an opportunity to bring practical necessities and moral requirements together to serve the common good."

—William A. Galston, Senior Fellow, Brookings Institution

"Hugh Heclo has written an eloquent defense of the enduring importance of authoritative institutions to human life, public and private. In an era suffused with so much noise, Heclo quietly reminds us that institutions serve that which is distinctively human, a life in community."

—**Jean Bethke Elshtain,** Laura Spelman Rockefeller Professor
of Social and Political Ethics, University of Chicago,
and author of *Democracy on Trial* and many other books

"This is truly a gem of a book: elegantly composed, artfully compressed, intellectually sparkling, and enduringly valuable. It is also a radical book, for it reaches down to the roots of things, challenging several centuries' worth of assumptions about the sufficiency of the individual and the soul-warping oppressiveness of institutions. Hugh Heclo demonstrates that such assumptions have always been half-truths at best, presuming the existence of the very things they would overturn. The paradox has only grown in recent years, for the more we have needed to rely on our institutions, the more we disparage them and seek to deny their necessary influence. Heclo's wise book is a compelling call to greater honesty and self-knowledge in these matters, both as individuals and as a nation. There is no American who would not benefit from reading it."

—**Wilfred M. McClay,** SunTrust Chair of Excellence
in Humanities, University of Tennessee at Chattanooga

"*On Thinking Institutionally* is a modern classic. Heclo has long been the outstanding scholar of American political institutions. Here he distills the insights and subtle understandings he has garnered over his long and distinguished career into a brief and lucid argument about how and why institutions matter and how one ought to think about them. I teach a course to first-year students entitled the Fundamentals of Politics. This book is of fundamental importance. Its key arguments can be grasped by them, and I very much look forward to assigning it to them."

—**Marc Landy**, Professor of Political Science, Boston College

"Hugh Heclo articulates the nature of the deep uneasiness gnawing at the heart of American culture more clearly and acutely than any other analyst I have read, and he points a way out of our present discontents. 'Wise' is not a word usually applied to social science, but *On Thinking Institutionally* merits it."

—**James Turner**, Cavanaugh Professor of Humanities,
University of Notre Dame

ON THINKING INSTITUTIONALLY

ON POLITICS

L. Sandy Maisel, Series Editor

On Politics is a new series of short reflections by major scholars on key subfields within political science. Books in the series are personal and practical as well as informed by years of scholarship and deliberation. General readers who want a considered overview of a field as well as students who need a launching platform for new research will find these books a good place to start. Designed for personal libraries as well as student backpacks, these smart books are small format, easy reading, aesthetically pleasing, and affordable.

Books in the Series

On the Presidency, Thomas E. Cronin
On Foreign Policy, Alexander L. George
On Media and Making Sense of Politics, Doris A. Graber
On Thinking Institutionally, Hugh Heclo
On Ordinary Heroes and American Democracy,
  Gerald M. Pomper

HUGH HECLO

ON THINKING
INSTITUTIONALLY

Paradigm Publishers

Boulder • London

Copyright © 2008 Paradigm Publishers

Published in the United States by Paradigm Publishers, 3360 Mitchell Lane, Suite E, Boulder, CO 80305 USA.

Paradigm Publishers is the trade name of Birkenkamp & Company, LLC, Dean Birkenkamp, President and Publisher.

Library of Congress Cataloging-in-Publication Data

Heclo, Hugh.
　On thinking institutionally / Hugh Heclo.
　　　p. cm. — (On politics)
　Includes bibliographical references and index.
　ISBN 13: 978-1-59451-263-7 (hardcover : alk paper)
1. Social institutions. 2. Values. I. Title.
　HM826.H43 2008
　306—dc22

　　　　　　　　　　　　　　　　2007052423

Printed and bound in the United States of America on acid-free paper that meets the standards of the American National Standard for Permanence of Paper for Printed Library Materials.

Designed and Typeset by Cheryl Hoffman.

12 11 10 09 08　　　1 2 3 4 5

CONTENTS

Acknowledgments, ix

1	Introduction: Respect for the Game	1
2	Our Modern Impasse	11
3	From Thinking about Institutions to Thinking Institutionally	45
4	Being Institutionally Minded	81
5	Applications, Dangers, and the Uphill Journey	129
6	Ways of Thinking, Ways of Being	185
Notes		197
Appendix: Selected Works of Hugh Heclo		215
Index		217
About the Author		221

ACKNOWLEDGMENTS

This book began as a lecture inflicted on an unsuspecting audience at Boston College in 2006. Although their names are unknown to me, I am grateful to the young students in the audience that autumn eve. Their astute questions and hopeful comments encouraged me to think there should be a book on this subject. Since then I have benefited greatly from the critical comments of persons kind enough to read all or parts of the resulting manuscript. My thanks to Christopher Bruell, James Ceaser, Martha Derthick, Robert Faulkner, Michael Lacey, Marc Landy, Stephan Leibfried, L. Sandy Maisel, James Pfiffner, and Don Wolfensberger.

CHAPTER ONE
INTRODUCTION:
RESPECT FOR THE GAME

Imagine two players in whatever your favorite sport might be. Both have the sort of extraordinary athletic gifts that you and I can only dream about. As with all great athletes, both players have a passionate competitive spirit and overwhelming desire to win. And both polish their gifts for this sport with relentless practice and training.

But with all that in common, there are some important differences between these two athletic stars. Let us call them Barry and Cal. Barry is a flashy personality intent on breaking records and given to dramatic acts of self-expression. He revels in the spotlight. Cal by contrast is quieter and more steady, almost businesslike in his approach to the game. He seems generally unimpressed by the celebrity status his talent has produced.

If we ask to whom or to what they hold themselves responsible, the answers in the end would be different. Barry sees himself as responsible to his fans, the record books, but ultimately to himself. Cal might express some similar views, but at the end of the day he would consider his ultimate obligation to be to the sport itself. One way of putting it is that Barry is "into" succeeding in his athletic career, and Cal is "into" succeeding in the game.

What does that mean? If we probed their thinking, we would find that their concepts of the "the game" itself are significantly different. For Barry the game is a setting in which his athletic prowess is exercised and his accomplishments are recorded. For Cal, the game is that whole rich tradition of people and events that defines his appropriate performance. Where Barry sees a set of rules, Cal sees an ethos. If he were philosophically inclined, Cal might say that the formal rules are "only the outer shell of the game. It is the history of the game—its sustaining traditions, lively passions, storied commitments, and evolving standards of excellence—that flesh-in this shell and enliven it as the specific kind of human practice that it is."[1]

Should we say it is just a matter of one person's being a team player and the other not? No, there is something deeper. Barry is intensely competitive and makes every effort to help his team win. But Cal appears to play for something more than his team. He hustles on every play even when his team is so far behind that there is no realistic chance of their winning a particular game.

Might we then say that the difference between Barry and Cal is one of intrinsic versus extrinsic rewards? Not really, because the fact is that both players seem to be getting both kinds of rewards. In terms of extrinsic rewards, both players certainly do value the big money, fan approval, and other perks that go with their status. In terms of intrinsic rewards, both love what they are doing. The difference is what they love about what they are doing. For Barry it is the love of his own sports accomplishments. For Cal, it is a matter of loving the game itself.

Of course, I have been describing two extremes, and any human being contains far more complex shadings than I am portraying in the persons of Barry and Cal. But if we are willing to focus on central tendencies and patterns of behavior, the contrast does have substance. The two players may be imaginary, but they point to something real. We know that is so simply by consulting our own experience. Across the landscape of contemporary sports, from the top professional ranks and filtering down to the local playground, there is ample testimony that things have been moving in the direction of the Barrys of this world and away from the Cals. The most obvious signs are the pervasive strutting, temper tantrums, trash talk, showboating, and other forms of public preening throughout the sports world. These and related tendencies have prompted a spate of efforts to rehabilitate ethical coaching, fair play, and sportsmanship in general.[2] But in contemporary society we seem to have trouble articulating what it is we are trying to rehabilitate.

It is clear enough that Barry's approach is essentially self-referential. But what shall we say about Cal's approach? Obviously, it is something more than self-referential. There is a positive quality that goes well beyond simply tamping down the fires of self-esteem, but how do we put into words what that something more is? The Cals of the world may find it difficult to say more than that they are just doing what a person in this sport is supposed to do. For example, listen to the Chicago Cubs' Ryne Sandberg at his 2005 induction speech to the Baseball Hall of Fame:

> I was in awe every time I walked onto the field. That's respect. I was taught you never, ever disrespect your opponent or your teammates or your organization or your manager and never, ever your uniform. Make a great play, act like you've done it before; get a big hit, look for the third base coach and get ready to run the bases; hit a home run, put your head down, drop the bat, run around the bases, because the name on the front is a lot more important than the name on the back. That's respect. . . . When did it become okay for someone to hit home runs and forget how to play the rest of the game? . . . These guys sitting up here [in the Baseball Hall of Fame] did not pave the way for the rest of us so that players could swing for the fences every time up and forget how to move a runner over to third. It's disrespectful to them, to you, and to the game of baseball that we all played growing up. Respect. A lot of people say this honor today validates my career, but I didn't work hard for validation. I didn't play the game right because I saw a reward at the end of the tunnel. I played it right because that's what you're supposed to do, play it right and with respect. . . . If this validates anything, it's that guys who taught me the game did what they were supposed to do and I did what I was supposed to do.[3]

The notion of "respect" provides a good point of entree into the subject of this little book. Sandberg's comments about respect are referring to something that goes beyond being especially polite toward teammates, coaches, opponents, or officials. Any such respectful attitude is an offshoot of the main thing. The root of the matter is a deeper and encompassing regard for the whole inherited tradition that makes up the game. In this deeper sense, respect is not about "niceness." It is about the player's sense of commitment to the entire social practice that is the game.

And yet, as you can sense from Sandberg's words, the language I have just used is too impersonal, too abstract. The essential human relationship is missing. Sandberg's words are expressing what should be called *respect-in-depth*. This is a respect that engages a person's sense of obligation to a community of living and dead people who embody the essence of this particular sport. Such respect entails a deferential regard for something beyond one's self. In this way of thinking, self-esteem is esteeming something too small. One's viewpoint needs to be expanded and elevated. To respect-in-depth is to honor something through your own appropriate participation in its practice.

Here lies the point of contact between the notion of respect and what are called institutional values. It is one thing to think about a sport. Both Barry and Cal do that. It is another thing to honor a sport by entering into its institutional tradition, thinking from inside its thinking, living it from the inside out, so to speak. In this introductory way we can say that respect for the game amounts to thinking institutionally. Later there will be more to say on this matter of "thinking about" versus "thinking within" institutions.

For now, it is sufficient to recognize that this subject invites us to consider not simply sports but also relationships woven throughout the daily texture of our lives. Thinking institutionally is not a purely intellectual exercise. It is a mixture of cognition and emotional attachment yielding habits of action. It is also a subject that invites us to render judgments about other people and, not least, about ourselves. To paraphrase Aristotle, Who is your hero and deserver of honor—the person who simply obtains the approval of others because of significant achievements, or the person who exercises virtues that sustain excellence in some social practice?

A major problem in considering this subject is that we are trying to talk about something that we experience mainly as an absence in modern public life. In one area after another, in-depth respect for the particular game in question often appears to be an afterthought. One might say about institutional thinking, "I know it when I don't see it." And there are an abundance of places where we do not see it.

In the realm of journalism, there are the obvious examples of Jayson Blair at the *New York Times,* Jack Kelley at *USA Today,* or Dan Rather at CBS, bending or breaking the rules of news-gathering. Or there is the example of *Newsweek* journalist Joe Klein publicly lying for six months about his authorship of the book *Primary Colors,* and growing in celebrity status as a result. But the issue goes beyond particular individuals. On the larger scene we see news organizations more invested in entertainment and celebrity reporters than in researching worthwhile news stories.

In business, the careers of once-celebrated leaders such as Al Dunlap at Sunbeam, Bernie Ebbers at WorldCom, and Ken Lay at Enron lie in ruins. However, outright criminality is only a small part of the matter. In the background are the less dramatic but more common stories of U.S. firms chasing a short-term bottom line at the expense of their employees and the long-term health of their companies.[4]

In professional sports, we have had to endure the showboating of individual athletes who, in their own minds, are already in their own private hall of fame. But beyond that, we have had to live through steroid and other scandals that represent much more than individual misdeeds. We have seen the collective failure of clubs, players' associations, sports commissions—in short corrupt if not criminal behavior by the very organizations that were supposed to uphold the integrity of the game in question.

Contemporary politics provides its own wealth of examples wherein leaders have ruined their own cause with sales jobs and other ostensibly "smart" moves that undermined the trust needed for eventual success.[5] It is the manner of leadership imprinted on the disastrous U.S. wars in Vietnam and Iraq. But again, it is more than a matter of individual leaders. In the political society as a whole, we are witnessing an absence of institutional thinking when politicians blithely mortgage our financial and environmental future, and citizens generally go along with such fiduciary malfeasance in order to be told what they want to hear.

In recent times the U.S. military has enjoyed high levels of public trust. But here too the same short-term thinking at the expense of long-term institutional values has come into public view. Let us leave aside the controversies over torture, military tribunals, or Abu Ghraib prison. We now know that senior officials manufactured false stories to turn Jessica Lynch into an unwilling heroine of the Iraq War and football star Pat Tillman into the leader of a courageous charge against the terrorists in an Afghan mountain pass, even though it was clear on the scene that he was killed by one of his own men.[6] The result of such machinations is a short burst of favorable publicity and long-term loss of credibility.

The institution I know best is the American university, and here there are plenty of examples, although they remain mostly hidden from public view. At the nation's ostensibly premier university, a brilliant new president lasts barely five years before resigning amid internal mistrust and dissension. At the same place, experts advising on reform in post-Communist Russia manage their own Institute for International Development into financial and moral collapse.[7] But here too, we should look beyond individual troubles to the broader picture. Critics can find abundant evidence of universities subordinating their long-term educational mission to immediate demands of the economic marketplace and student consumers.[8] Likewise, the professionals trained in our elite institutions of higher learning often acquire the technical expertise for personal success without a sense of the normative good at the heart of their professional identities as lawyers, doctors, teachers, and the like.[9]

My point is this. Lies, short-term thinking, self-promotion, denigration of duty, disregard for larger purposes—all these amount to one common syndrome serving to undermine social trust and institutional values. The names of particular persons and organizations fade from our memory, only to be replaced by the next day's news of scandal and shortsighted stupidity. A lack of institutional thinking may not be the whole story, but there is a common thread in a great deal of the dysfunctional behavior we see in one sphere of contemporary life after another. That thread is about people neglecting and dishonoring the longer-term values of the going concern of which they are a part.

Such an approach to life is even glamorized as something to celebrate and emulate. Today's popular culture devotes vast amounts of attention and money to the star power of ephemeral personal success. The message is: become a celebrity or else be sidelined as just another drudging worker bee. In the same way, we are besieged by a consumer culture promoting a short-term self-preoccupation. This self is portrayed as being in a continuously needy condition, capable of affirming itself only by acquiring an ever-mounting array of material and symbolic goods. As one cultural critic observed, it is "a quivering, sentimental self that gets uncomfortable very quickly, because this self has to feel good about itself all the time. Such selves do not make good arguments. They validate one another."[10]

It is easy to chronicle widespread disregard for institutional values. And yet there is also a hopeful aspect to all of this. In their everyday lives people do retain the capacity to be offended by behavior that undermines the integrity of public and private institutions—behavior that "stinks up the game." Later there will be more to say about this widespread but mostly unarticulated understanding of the value of institutional values. Let me simply note here that when a person, as in the case of Ryne Sandberg, has to explain his loyalty to a thing beyond the self, something unnatural has already occurred.

Sometimes, rather than seeing its absence, we catch a positive glimpse of the thing itself. In these instances we can sense an essential appropriateness in someone's way of thinking and acting. It is what we saw in Sherron Watkins and Cynthia Cooper, vice presidents at Enron and WorldCom, respectively, who fought against the improper accounting practices that eventually brought down those companies and major accounting firms. We saw it in Coleen Rowley, the FBI field office attorney who tried to make her organization recognize its failure to respond to evidence of terrorist activity prior to 9/11. As Rowley wrote to the FBI director, "The issues are fundamentally ones of integrity and go to the heart of the FBI's law enforcement mission and mandate."[11]

The same institutionalist perspective was displayed by Alberto Mora, general counsel of the U.S. Navy who tried to stop the disastrous policy that sanctioned cruelty during interrogation of terrorist suspects, something he recognized as unlawful and unworthy of America's military services. When the abuses Mora foresaw surfaced over a year later at Abu Ghraib prison in Iraq, it was another upholder of institutional values, Army Major General Antonio Taguba, who fought against his military and political superiors to produce an honest investigation. Why take on that uphill fight? As Taguba put it, "From the moment a soldier enlists, we inculcate loyalty, duty, honor, integrity, and selfless service. And yet when we get to the senior-officer level we forget those values. … The fact is that we violated the laws of land warfare in Abu Ghraib. We violated the tenets of the Geneva Convention. We violated our own principles, and we violated the core of our military values."[12]

Essentially, these were people simply doing what they were supposed to do in order to uphold the values of their profession and their organizations' larger purposes. In the short run they damaged their careers. In the long run they stood up for personal and institutional integrity. As we shall see, thinking and acting institutionally is something that normally occurs in less dramatic circumstances. Nevertheless, such extreme examples can help reassure us that in talking about business enterprises, journalism, sports, higher education, the rule of law, or any social practice at its "truest and best," we are talking about something real, that there really is an institutional soul to sustain or lose.

The messages of the popular culture tell us one thing. The lessons from ordinary life—if we take time to think about them—tell us something else. And it turns out that the lessons from what we see in daily life have a commonsense wisdom that rings true. Striving to make yourself the celebrity star in your own life leaves you striving in an empty house of mirrors. Has the satisfaction proven to be just out of reach? Like the Great Gatsby, has the dream eluded us so far? "That's no matter— tomorrow we will run faster, stretch out our arms farther. ... And one fine morning ..."[13]

The wisdom of daily experience tells us something different. The deeper satisfactions we crave come from strong bonds of mutual attachment to other people and larger causes outside ourselves. Then the mirrors become windows and doors into a wider world of loyalties. In that world a sense of well-being and happiness finds us rather than our frantically chasing it down. It is a place where a person has a chance to find the simple satisfaction that comes from doing a job the way it is supposed to be done. It is a place where enduring relationships can liberate us from self-preoccupation, where we gain by giving of ourselves. It is here, not in the glare of celebrity, that life gains an authentic sparkle. And while the popular culture might not notice or reward these larger loyalties, they are the kind of things you and I are likely to cherish when, from some terminus, we look back on the course our lives have taken.[14]

Something deep inside us seems to recognize the dysfunctional, unsatisfactory quality of an anti-institutional way of living. Inwardly we know that institutional values and commitments are important. But in contemporary society it is difficult to find a vocabulary and grammar for even beginning to talk about such an old-fashioned subject. When it comes to the idea of thinking institutionally, we as modern people have reached a befogged impasse, and our public and private lives show it. This book is an effort at recovery and articulation on behalf of that unfashionable idea.

CHAPTER TWO
OUR MODERN IMPASSE

We are disposed to distrust institutions. That is the basic fact of life we share as modern people. And it is the point of departure from which this account must begin. As good pluralists, tolerant multiculturalists, secular or religious moralists (choose your term), we can be divided on almost any other imaginable subject. But a fundamental distrust of institutions is the one mark we have in common as inhabitants of these times.

Of course, not everyone is actively distrustful of every institution all the time. If that were the case, we would not have a functioning society. Media impressions to the contrary, we do have such a society. The distrust of institutions is not so much an active rejection as a prevailing disposition, a fixed slant in our frame of reference. To be sure, most of the time we do not bother our heads about the subject. And there are good, practical reasons why we pay little attention to the larger institutional structures and processes within which we spend our daily lives. But comes an incident or piece of news, and we nod in agreement that "you just can't trust them."

It is that pervasive, recurrent nod of agreement we have in common as modern, twenty-first-century people. We are compelled to live in a thick tangle of institutions while believing that they do not have our best interests at heart. Like a disgruntled teenager, we are not quite willing to run away from home, but there is no mistaking the sullen malcontent in the house.

Political institutions are a striking example. Social scientists disagree on the details and explanations, but all agree on the general trend in the data from opinion surveys. Since the mid-twentieth century there has been a pervasive decline in Americans' trust in their national political institutions. While varying with particular events and personalities, the overall trend of growing distrust applies to the presidency, Congress, and federal government as a whole. It also appears that confidence in the Supreme Court as an institution has declined in recent years.[1]

None of this translates into an overt lack of support for the nation's constitutional form of government. Only a few oddballs will tell an interviewer that they do not believe in the U.S. Constitution. But the evidence does indicate a growing loss of faith that our political institutions are operating in the best interests of the American people. And that *does* amount to something resembling a covert loss of support for our constitutional system. It is saying that a great many citizens think the ongoing processes of our government (winning office, legislating, administering and so on) are failing to work for the institutional purpose intended—namely, to serve the interests of the people. At the beginning of 2005—before public reaction against the Iraq War, Hurricane Katrina, or major congressional scandals—barely a quarter of Americans expressed a great deal of trust in their elective national institutions to operate in the people's interest. Slightly over four in ten Americans expressed little or no such trust.[2]

Growing distrust is not confined to political institutions. In recent decades we modern people have grown more suspicious of almost all our society's major institutions. That includes business, unions, public schools, the legal and medical professions, religious institutions, journalism, and nonprofit organizations. With a few exceptions, growing distrust in the modern mind is directed toward the entire institutional apparatus of modern society. If you imagine that apparatus as a sort of bank, the overall picture is one of many withdrawals, few deposits, and a continuous depletion of trust reserves.[3]

Neither is this trend confined to the United States. Growing distrust of institutional authority can be found among virtually all the advanced nations of the world.[4] Good international survey data on this subject do not exist much before the beginning of the twenty-first century, but the general story it tells seems clear enough. Trust that major institutions are working in the best interests of society has been low and mostly declining across the developed world.

There is, of course, such a thing as healthy distrust, especially when it comes to people and institutional structures that have power over our lives. This is the doubt—the challenging and calling into question of power—that helps sustain a democracy and keeps it from running off the tracks into public gullibility.[5] Because citizens insist on raising questions, power holders are compelled to give reasons. However, it would be more accurate to call this healthy view by the name of doubt or skepticism. Skepticism is a matter of exercising our critical faculties to question others' claims and demand an accounting. The modern inclination to distrust typically goes beyond that. That institutional authority should be distrusted does not seem to be in doubt. The modern view expects the worst because it has already reached the conclusion that institutions and their leaders are generally oppressive and self-serving. This widespread view of the institutional apparatus that surrounds us is not critical or skeptical. The correct word for it is "cynical." Institutional authorities do not deserve the benefit of the doubt. What they deserve is mistrust. Case closed.

Or so it might seem. In a way there is something rather odd about our distrust of institutions, because it runs against the conservative grain of human nature. Across many centuries and cultures, there has been an enduring folk wisdom recommending a preference for the devil you know over the devil you do not know. During the last thirty years, social science research has greatly expanded this ancient insight into our human predisposition. Experiments at the intersection of economics and psychology have produced Nobel Prizes and a great deal of knowledge about how people make decisions in an uncertain world.

For the most part, people do not behave as posited by traditional economic theory. They do not seek to maximize their expected utility in choosing among different probable outcomes. Relative to some reference level (such as the status quo), people are much more averse to suffering losses than they are attracted by gains of the same size. People are disposed toward rootedness. There is a deep-seated asymmetry between our view of gains and losses, and it favors holding on to what we already have. For example, it appears that to compensate for a $10 loss requires a $25 gain in order for people to break even psychologically.[6] Such deep-seated loss aversion ought to work in favor of institutional allegiances. After all, institutions represent arrangements that we have inherited as part of the status quo and that are ours to lose. Institutions are the smooth, well-worn handles by which people have historically held on to and managed their social and political affairs. They must be some very powerful forces that could overcome our natural human aversion to loss, something able to make us inclined to distrust and let go of those handles. What might those forces be?

A general explanation for the widespread negative view of institutions can reasonably be divided into two parts, one lying in plain view with the daily news and the other residing in deeper cultural currents. In both parts of the explanation, I think it can be shown that alongside the cynicism directed toward institutions there is also a more positive but hidden subtext pointing toward institutional values. These positive hints give me hope that, even in our contemporary anti-institutionalist world, a book about thinking institutionally is not quite the fool's errand it might seem to be.

Performance-Based Distrust

In the first place, today's institutions have gained our distrust the old-fashioned way. They have earned it. We might call this performance-based distrust. It draws its power from the experience of millions of ordinary people hearing about all sorts of breaches of trust by those in positions of institutional authority. By now we are sufficiently desensitized that what follows might appear to be simply the ambient muck one expects to slog through if you are keeping up on current events.

What sort of muck? Let us confine ourselves to three core areas of social order—institutions of the private, public, and non-profit sectors. The evidence lies so thick around us that it might seem too obvious and tiresome to make a list. But I think there is probably no better way to gain an appreciation for the cumulative, relentless quality of what has happened. Bit by bit, incident by incident, daily life in the contemporary United States has been schooling us in the ways of distrust.

To trust private sector business institutions, we would have to be oblivious to the massive evidence of negligence, malfeasance, and outright criminality among business leaders that has accumulated in recent memory.[7] One could begin simply with corporate names that symbolize the betrayal of trust—names such as Adelphia, AIG Insurance, Investors Overseas Service, Cendant, Imclone, Global Crossings, Tyco, Phar-Mor, Kidder Peabody, HealthSouth, Sunbeam, Waste Management, WorldCom, Prudential Bache, and, of course, Enron, to name a few.

Beyond this are broader categories of institutional misconduct. Examples over the last twenty years include such costly messes as the "Savings and Loan scandal" (Charles Keating, Lincoln Savings and Loan, etc.), the "Junk Bond scandal" (Ivan Boesky, Michael Milken, Drexel Burnham Lambert, etc.), the "BCCI Money Laundering scandal" (ruining the public reputation of Clark Clifford, an esteemed advisor to four presidents), and the "Mutual Funds scandal" (widespread insider trading that cheated small investors in mutual funds run by Bank One,

Invesco, Janus Capital Group, Bank of America, Prudential Securities, and Putnam Investments, among other major financial
institutions). It does no good to say that these are just particular
individuals and organizations, not the whole business community. Bit by bit, drip by drip—that is the way any general sense of
trust is eroded.

By the first four years of the twenty-first century, essentially
all of the leading public accounting firms of the United States
(Arthur Andersen, Deloitte and Touche, Ernst and Young,
KPMG, PricewaterhouseCoopers) had admitted to negligence in
the execution of their duty or had paid substantial fines without
admitting guilt. In that same period, SEC investigations found
that every major investment bank in the United States (including Merrill Lynch, Goldman Sachs, Morgan Stanley, Citigroup,
First Boston, Lehman Brothers Holdings, J. P. Morgan, Chase)
had assisted efforts to defraud investors. Such efforts included
urging investors to buy shares in companies that the banks' own
analysts were privately describing as junk. For any insiders trying
to auction off their ill-gotten baubles, there might have been
rough justice, since around that same time Sotheby's and
Christie's auction houses (jointly controlling 90 percent of the
world's high-end auction market) were found to have engaged in
a multiyear price-fixing conspiracy, with Sotheby's chairman,
American billionaire Alfred Taubman, fined and sent to jail.

Arching beyond cases of outright criminality are the long-
running stories in which the common theme is one of dealing
in bad faith with the public. In those national stories, businesses
have sought to reassure people that DDT, asbestos, tobacco, and
a host of other dangerous materials are not really harmful. They
have hidden and then tried to explain away toxic waste dumps
such as Love Canal. Leading U.S. car makers have sought to
evade basic safety standards (a theme set in motion in the 1960s
and 1970s with the Chevrolet Corvair and Ford Pinto).

The strongest acid corroding trust has had nothing to do
with misconduct. It has stemmed from structural changes in the
economy that lie beyond anyone's control. After the 1960s,

growing competitive pressure in the national and worldwide markets has produced new rules of the game—rules that ordinary people experience as the declining loyalty of firms toward their employees and local communities. What business leaders have felt they have to do to achieve "good performance," economically understood, has typically been experienced as a performance failure by those dependent on those businesses. The growing sense of a more insecure economic future appears to have undermined Americans' general levels of trust.[8]

The issue here is not the merits of different sides in these particular controversies. The point is that since the 1960s there has been a steady drumbeat of experiences that would understandably drive a great many people in the direction of distrusting private-sector institutions.

If anything, the public sector has excelled even more in the teaching of distrust. Social scientists tell us that events occurring as people move through their early formative years of political consciousness have a lasting impact. Imagine that you began life as a member of the first cohort of the Baby Boom generation born in the immediate aftermath of World War II, America's last "good war." As a preteen in 1958, the clock of your political socialization will have begun ticking. Each subsequent cohort born after 1945 has joined with you seriatim and experienced all the subsequent items on the list of events set forth in Box 2.1. We might wish all of this were a bad dream. In fact, it is the outline of a lengthening curriculum teaching political distrust across the last two generations of Americans. To one degree or another, Box 2.1 shows us what everybody living today has had to live through and respond to regarding our political institutions. One incident or another might be dismissed. The cumulative weight cannot.

Although far from a complete listing, Box 2.1 provides a rough picture of the abuse our national political institutions had taken by the end of the twentieth century. It was a rare year in which there is not some major development exposing a betrayal of the public trust. Our mythical Baby Boomer came to political

Box 2.1 A Baby Boomer's Primer for Political Distrust

1958   Resignation of President Eisenhower's chief of staff, Sherman Adams, for accepting vicuña coat and other gifts from a business under investigation by the Federal Trade Commission.

1960   Downing of U-2 spy plane over Russia. Eisenhower administration's public statements are proven false when Russians unexpectedly produce the pilot and plane.

1961   Bay of Pigs. Washington officials falsely deny involvement in failed attempt to invade Cuba by CIA-trained exiles.

1962   Billy Sol Estes affair. Texas financier and political associate of Vice President Johnson convicted of fraud. Four other figures in the affair die of apparent suicide.

1963   Bobby Baker, longtime associate of Vice President Lyndon Johnson, resigns as secretary to the Senate majority amid charges of corruption and dealings with underworld figures.

1963   Assassination of President Kennedy. Beginning of conspiracy theories that continue to proliferate for the rest of the century.

1964   Congressional passage of the Gulf of Tonkin Resolution. False information supplied by President Johnson is used as a pretext for expanding U.S. engagement in the Vietnam War.

1967   Civil rights leader Adam Clayton Powell, Jr., of New York is expelled from Congress, then reelected.

        Senator Thomas J. Dodd is censured for financial misconduct and corruption.

1968   Growth of conspiracy theories following the assassinations of Martin Luther King, Jr., and Bobby Kennedy.

1969   Supreme Court Associate Justice Abe Fortas resigns amid financial scandal revealed during his nomination to become Chief Justice.

1969–   After campaigning on the promise to end the
1970   Vietnam War with honor, President Nixon initiates secret bombing of Cambodia and invasions of Laos. Nixon's public announcement of the invasion of Cambodia in April

	1970 produces nationwide protests, including Kent State shooting deaths of four students.
1971– 1972	Pentagon Papers. Leaked Defense Department report shows that the Johnson Administration secretly expanded the Vietnam War while publicly promising not to do so.
1972– 1974	Watergate. In the press and then in dramatic nationally televised Senate hearings, a growing revelation of abuses of power and illegal cover-ups at the highest levels of the Nixon administration.
1973	Financial scandal and resignation of Vice President Spiro Agnew.
1974	Resignation of President Nixon, with full pardon granted by incoming President Ford.
1975– 1976	Senate Select (Church) Committee documents illegal activities and abuses of power by the FBI and CIA throughout World War II period.
1977	Resignation of President Carter's budget director Bert Lance amid allegations of misuse of funds. Tongsun Park, working as an agent for South Korea, is convicted of bribing members of Congress along with other crimes.
1980	Abscam scandal. FBI sting operation leads to the conviction of one senator and five congressmen on conspiracy and bribery charges.
1981	President Reagan's budget director, David Stockman, reveals that the administration's landmark tax cut and budget legislation were intentionally deceptive in their strategy and budget projections.
1983	Congressional page scandal. Two congressmen censured by the House for having sexual relations with seventeen-year-old pages.
1986– 1997	Iran-Contra affair. Officials in the Reagan administration assist in illegal sales of military weapons to Iran as well as illegal transfer of the sale proceeds to right-wing insurgents in Nicaragua. President Reagan at first denies that such arms sales occurred but then affirms the

transfer of weapons to Iran while denying that they were part of an exchange for hostages held in Lebanon.

1987   Bork nomination. In nationally televised hearings, Robert Bork's nomination to the Supreme Court is defeated in the most viciously contested confirmation fight in living memory.

1988   Wedtech scandal. Independent counsel shows that Wedtech used insider influence to fraudulently acquire no-bid defense contracts. The attorney general and several top members of the Reagan White House are implicated, two congressmen are forced to resign, and more than a dozen federal, state, and local officials are convicted of related crimes.

1989   Senator John Tower's nomination as defense secretary is defeated following allegations of alcohol abuse, womanizing, and improper ties to the defense industry.

House Speaker Jim Wright is forced to resign after an ethics committee investigation finds multiple violations of House rules.

1989– 1990   Keating Five scandal. Five senators are found to have improperly tried to interfere with law enforcement efforts in the savings and loan industry while receiving political contributions from businesses under investigation.

1990   House Majority Whip Anthony Lee Coelho retires after revelations of unethical practices involving savings and loan and junk bond deals.

Senator David Durenberger, chairman of the Select Committee on Intelligence, is denounced by the Senate for unethical conduct.

1991   Clarence Thomas nomination. After a bitter partisan fight over Thomas's qualifications to replace Thurgood Marshall, confirmation hearings explode on national television regarding Anita Hill's charges of sexual harassment.

1991– 1995   Congressional post office scandal. Charges of embezzlement and other misconduct lead to the criminal conviction of House Ways and Means Committee Chairman Dan Rostenkowski and the congressional postmaster, among others.

1992	House banking scandal. Most House members are shown to benefit from special privileges outside normal banking rules. Four former congressmen, the D.C. delegate, and the former House sergeant-at-arms are convicted of criminal wrongdoing.
	Outgoing President George H. W. Bush pardons Casper Weinberger and five other Iran-Contra figures days before their criminal trials are to begin.
1992– 2000	Whitewater. Protracted investigations and multiple charges of illegality involving land deal financing by the Clintons during the 1980s. Eventually several Clinton friends, business associates, the governor of Arkansas, and a municipal judge are convicted. Final report of Independent Counsel Ray concludes that there is insufficient evidence to prove that President or Mrs. Clinton had committed any crime.
1993	White House Travel Office scandal. Charging financial misconduct, President Clinton fires seven longtime employees of the office. The resulting controversy leads to reinstatement of most employees and redirection of travel office business from Clinton's business friends. An independent counsel's final report concludes that Hillary Clinton had made factually false statements but that there was insufficient evidence for prosecution.
	President Clinton's first two choices for attorney general withdraw after revelations of employing illegal aliens.
	Suicide of White House lawyer and childhood Clinton friend Vince Foster produces new round of unsubstantiated conspiracy theories.
1994	Webster Hubbell scandal. Associate U.S. attorney general, former chief justice of the Arkansas Supreme Court, and close Clinton friend pleads guilty to federal mail fraud and tax evasion.
1995	Federal government shutdown. A political impasse over budget negotiations between President Clinton and House Speaker Newt Gingrich results in the first cessation of nonessential services in the federal government, to the disgust of the general public.

1996	Filegate. The White House Office of Personnel Security is found to have improperly obtained FBI background files on hundreds of former employees from the Bush and Reagan administrations. Political operative heading the office resigns.
1997	House Speaker Gingrich is reprimanded and fined by the House for financial improprieties.
1998	Speaker Gingrich resigns from the House after Republican call for Clinton's impeachment produces losses in the midterm congressional election.
	During debate on the Clinton impeachment resolution, new House Speaker–elect Bob Livingston resigns after evidence of his own sexual indiscretions surfaces in response to *Hustler* magazine's offer to pay up to $1 million for such information about Republican leaders.
1998– 1999	President Clinton is impeached for perjury and obstruction of justice in connection with the Paula Jones sexual harassment case, in which he falsely testified that he did not have sexual relations with White House intern Monica Lewinsky. The president is acquitted in the Senate trial by a mainly party-line vote.

consciousness with reports of an ill-gotten vicuña coat hanging in the White House and approached retirement age amid presidential claims that oral sex is not a form of "sexual relations." Of course, the list has continued to lengthen in Washington during more recent years, but there is no need here to review those unhappy events.

As with the private sector, so too with government institutions there is an aspect of performance-based distrust that has been of a larger, more structural character. The agenda on which government performance is expected to be judged expanded in a stunning way after the late 1950s. In the course of a single generation, the reputation of our political institutions was put on the line to achieve fundamental improvements in more or less every facet of human life. This included education at all levels, poverty, urban redevelopment, health care, comprehensive environmental protection, racial justice, gender equality, and all aspects of consumer safety. It was as if a person barely adept at performing the necessities of daily life were asked to undertake the Olympic decathlon. Judgments of performance by the new welfare state necessarily suffered.

Some have looked to the so-called third sector of non-governmental organizations (NGOs) as a corrective for the excesses of big government and freewheeling capitalism. And yet the rapidly expanding world of NGOs has presented the public with its own cavalcade of trust-draining experiences. Perhaps the two most prominent "nonprofit" organizations in the United States are the United Way and Red Cross; both have helped to undermine public confidence. In the early 1990s, the United Way's longtime CEO, William Aromony, and two other top officials were convicted of stealing from the charity to support lavish lifestyles. Despite a new code of ethics and accountability procedures, exposés of financial misconduct have been repeated in local chapters such as Washington, D.C. (whose CEO was convicted of stealing nearly a half-million dollars from the charity and its pension fund in 2004), and New York (whose CEO was shown to have misappropriated charity assets from 2002 to 2005). Other local United Ways have been accused of inflating overhead charges, double-counting contributions, and other improprieties.[9]

For years critics had charged the Red Cross with exploiting disasters to obtain donations that were then reallocated to other operations of the organization, including paying for fund-raising. Cases in point were the San Francisco earthquake (1989), Oklahoma City bombing (1995), and San Diego fire (2001). It took the 9/11 terrorist attacks to drive the point home. In the immediate aftermath of this disaster the Red Cross quickly raised more than half a billion dollars with the promise that all 9/11 donations would go to victims of the attacks. Subsequent congressional investigations revealed that roughly half of the donations had been reallocated to other operations of the Red Cross organization. The resignation of the Red Cross's head, Dr. Bernadine Healy, soon followed.

Scholars have reviewed the broader range of NGO wrong-doings that began to be reported in the news media in the 1990s. Motivated by greed and perceived entitlement, most of these incidents occurred over a lengthy period, reflected a lack of institutional oversight, and had negative long-term effects on the organization in question.[10] In a larger sense, all such seemingly disconnected incidents have left a durable imprint of public mistrust. A Brookings Institution study found that by 2004 only 15 percent of Americans had a great deal of confidence in nonprofit organizations, a roughly 10 to 15 percent drop from three years earlier. Only 19 percent of Americans thought that nonprofits ran their programs well, and just 11 percent believed that charities spent money wisely. Overall, Americans continue to have significantly less confidence in charities than they did before the 9/11 terrorist attacks.[11]

One could go on to talk about religious institutions, where Protestant and Catholic churches alike have been damaged by high-level clerical misconduct. Or we might look at legal institutions, where sensationalized cases on television, political agendas in the courts, and professional misconduct among lawyers have helped to undermine confidence in the rule of law. The grounds for performance-based distrust can be found all around us. Wading through all of this material will likely leave a person with a strong sense of needing to take a shower.

Still, I think it important to have spent time in the preceding few pages recounting the sad record. We easily become desensitized and distracted by the passing parade of daily events and miss the larger picture of what has been happening to us. Of course, the preceding survey of lowlights should be kept in perspective. As the list itself demonstrates, abuses were discovered (though what proportion of the potential total no one knows). Misconduct was punished. Some reforms have been instituted. Financial markets, businesses, NGOs, political and other institutions have continued to function, and probably in most cases to function appropriately.

The point for our purposes is the collective impact of such disclosures on any normal citizen's perception of the surrounding world of institutions. It would be silly to think that many people remember the details from the laundry list of misdeeds I have recounted. It would be just as silly to think that the recurring disclosures of institutional betrayals of trust have not had a cumulative effect on people's views.[12] Given a choice of bestowing trust or distrust, should we really be surprised if ordinary citizens incline toward cynicism? In light of the cumulative record, anyone would seem a fool to do otherwise.

It might be objected that it is the leaders running various institutions and not the institutions themselves in which people lose confidence.[13] At a given moment this distinction may make sense, but over any significant period of time the performance of leaders and the performance of institutions are inextricably bound together. Institutional failure, and the distrust it engenders, is the result of people continually failing to live up to legitimate expectations attached to their positions of responsibility. After all, institutions as such are simply a mental abstraction. When institutions fail it is living, breathing human beings and not mental abstractions that fail.

In that light one might protest that my account of performance failures presupposes a too high-minded and unrealistic view of the subject. Such a critic would say that what I have described is only human nature. The best response to this lame complacency is a paraphrase of Katherine Hepburn's retort to the cynicism of Humphrey Bogart's character in *The African Queen:* human nature, Mr. Allnutt, is what we put institutions in this world to rise above. Precisely because men are not angels, we turn to institutions and their standards to help restrain and channel our ordinary human impulses to lie, cheat, and steal (among other numerous faults that come naturally to our species). When institutions become venues for expressing—and even facilitating—greed, lust, cowardice, and selfishness, we are not seeing something "natural." We are seeing something debauched.

So then, has institutional leadership become more venal, misguided and debauched in recent decades than it was in the past? I have no way of knowing that, and as far as I can tell neither does anyone else. In the next chapter we will discuss some remarkable institutional insights displayed in the founding of our nation. But the historical record is probably too thoroughly sordid to support any simple claim of a lost Golden Age.

What I think is demonstrably true is that in the last two generations or so, the normal range and frequency of human failings have presented themselves to the public in new ways, ways that possess an especially corrosive power in matters of institutional trust. To put it in other words, even if human venality and other misconduct remained constant, we have lived through a period when the betrayal of trust has become formatted in such a manner as to magnify whatever public alienation would have otherwise occurred. That is what sets the last half-century apart in generating performance-based distrust. To appreciate why this is so, we might subdivide the modern formatting innovations into three categories.

First is what might be called the *scale effect*. Given the technology available to him, Charles Ponzi had to work hard in 1920 to defraud about 40,000 people. In our time, modern communications and other technologies of social organization have made it possible to carry out institutional misconduct on a vast, complex scale affecting masses of people at the same time. At the beginning of the twenty-first century, the litigation settlement for only one brokerage firm (Merrill Lynch) in the larger stock market scandal involved more than two dozen companies and millions of investors. Most of the work to carry off this betrayal of trust involved nothing more than some clicks on a computer mouse. In that sense the new capacity for generating institutional distrust is comparable to the situation regarding contemporary school violence or terrorism. Replacing clubs, knives, and single-action guns with weaponry capable of mass destruction, technology has exponentially expanded the public impact of what any misguided individual or group might do.

Second, there is a *display effect* that vastly magnifies our perceptions of institutional failure. In 1922, Walter Lippman marked how the press served up a dramatized picture of "news" and "stereotypes," creating the pictures in our heads that shape our public life. For all of Lippman's insight, that was just a tiny foretaste of the world we would enter after 1950 (when only about one in ten American households had a television). What we have created since then is an immense, pervasive system of communications providing not only the pictures but also the processes and commentaries trying to tell the public what it thinks. Because this system is the sea of social interpretation we swim in, we hardly notice it by now. Scandals and other examples of poor institutional performance are sought out, dramatically packaged, instantly communicated, and incessantly repeated for mass public consumption.[14]

Of course, the display is hardly representative. Almost none of the extraordinary common things of life are ever considered newsworthy. Yet if you think about it, one of the most remarkable things in the world is that great hosts of people are going about doing their jobs and enabling all sorts of institutions to work properly. They are like the planes taking off and landing hundreds of times a day in thousands of places. Ostensibly, nothing much "happens," but that is because everyone is mostly doing what they are supposed to be doing to make things happen right. And it all passes right by us. In its place are the crash-and-burn stories from which we take our cues and readings about the state of things in the world.

Finally, those cues and readings are all now colored by what can be called a *PR effect*. By that I mean the professionalized sell-job that characterizes every sphere of interaction between institutional authorities and the public and—more important—people's recognition of that pervasive fact. This magnifying effect on institutional distrust is less obvious than the first two and deserves a little more consideration.

At the time when Lippman wrote and Ponzi schemed, professional public relations had barely begun to distinguish itself from the publicity stuntmen and hucksters of the pre–World War I United States. By the 1930s corporate America had begun to support a growing, professionalized, and well-paid public relations and marketing industry, in large part to burnish its Depression-scarred public image. By the 1950s the first crossovers from this private-sector PR industry into political PR marketing began to occur.[15] The wholesale penetration of television into U.S. homes accelerated the process. By the time the first Baby Boomers began approaching adulthood in the 1960s, entrenchment of a professionally managed system of public communications was well under way, and it has been consolidating itself throughout society ever since.

This professional selling in public communications now covers a range of specialized services we take for granted as the way of doing business with the public. They include scientific polling, focus group and other market research, strategic communications planning, image and news event management, advertising production and media buys, damage control, fundraising, direct mail, and "spontaneous" grassroots mobilization, as well as supplying Internet content and marketing. For any major activity in the public, private, or nonprofit sectors, the apparatus of persuasion seeks to cover every point of contact with the public. It is like an oil slick, coating everything it touches and imparting a pervasive guile to the conduct of our public business. Idealistic founders of the PR industry such as Elmer Roper had thought they would be experts advising clients how to *deserve* the public's approval.[16] In practice, the vast infrastructure that developed is concentrated merely on how to obtain and mold it to suit one's interests.

The point is not just that public communications has become public relations. The larger issue is that the public knows it. One reason we know it is that the display effect continually reports stories revealing the professional "spinning" that seeks to shape our perceptions. A deeper reason is that ordinary people have common sense. What they experience in the PR effect is not straightforward lying. What people have become aware of is a nonstop effort at seduction in which the truth is essentially irrelevant. Projecting an image of "truthiness" is how "they" try to make us see things their way.

Ordinary citizens, who are more perceptive than professional spinners think, can sense the phoniness in the way their would-be seducers talk to them. Here is a short list of some prevailing strategies used by today's professionals in public communications:

- Stay on a simple message (rather than dealing with complex realities).
- Appeal to emotions (rather than taking time to reason with the audience).
- "Frame" issues to steer people toward the desired conclusion (rather than informing them about the substance of any given issue).
- Project self-assurance (rather than admitting uncertainty or ignorance).
- Counterattack or switch the subject (rather than trying to answer tough questions).
- Avoid self-criticism (rather than trying to correct your errors).
- Claim to have the whole answer (rather than admitting there is any independent expertise that is not on your side).
- Above all, talk to win (rather than to get at the truth of things).

While this list is my distillation, it is not my invention. These are prevailing norms in our modern process of public communications. The results are sham debates, crude "message"-sending, a pro-wrestling version of democratic discourse that insults the intelligence of any self-respecting adult. Ordinary citizens on the receiving end of the persuasion industry have every reason to believe that public life is a spin cycle where nobody ever comes clean.

So what does the PR effect have to do with institutional distrust? To find the answer, we might return to the preceding short list and imagine two acquaintances. One deals with you in the terms indicated at the beginning of each bullet and the other does so along the lines contained in the parentheses. Once you realize you are the target of a sell-job, trust goes out the window. It's time to keep your hand on your wallet. More than that, the rhetorical tricks, focus group–tested talking points, and slick strategies are a way of saying that you are not being taken seriously.

Hence the paradox: the more professional and adept our leaders have become in plying the persuasive arts, the more distrustful their audience has become. Of course, it is no paradox at all but simply an expression of an ancient law of human affairs.[17] We come to distrust those who distrust us. Indirectly, our salesmen/leaders demonstrate that they do not trust us to be able to handle the truth, and we reciprocate their disdain.

Put together the *scale, display,* and *PR* effects. Add the list of actual misdeeds in the public, private, and nonprofit sectors over the last two generations. No surprise: we arrive at the central, takeaway lesson. "They" are not to be trusted. This seems the only really sensible stance toward the institutional world we are forced to inhabit. To distrust those in positions of institutional authority is to be a savvy, sophisticated person. Such a person not only refuses to be taken in by statements of good intentions. He or she also realizes that there are no such things as good intentions. There are only power relationships. All sincerity is strategy; all communications are layered with self-serving calculation. As this sensibility takes hold, people will naturally no longer feel that they should believe what institutional authorities tell them or do what such authorities ask of them—which of course means that they are not seen as institutional authorities at all but as mere powerbrokers.

If people were wholly captive to the industry of the spin-meisters, they would surely be too deluded to register their prevailing high levels of institutional distrust. Ordinary people seem more offended than enchanted by their world of public persuasion. But from where is this capacity to be offended coming? What must be true for us to take offense in the first place? At this point a glimmer of light comes into view. The cynicism comes easily to us. But pause to look more deeply and you can see something more.

If average citizens are scandalized by all I have been describing, it is because they implicitly know something very important. They know that while those in positions of institutional authority may repeatedly fail to meet our expectations, to fail to hold on to those expectations would be even more disastrous. The fact is that most people apparently believe that there really are institutional standards of proper performance. That is what makes it possible for our institutions and their leaders to disappoint us. But it goes beyond disappointment.

A CEO misleading investors with false reassurances, a president shaving the English language to communicate bald-faced half-truths, a doctor performing unnecessary procedures on patients to collect larger fees—such things will rightly produce reactions in us that go beyond disappointment or regret for the specific misdeed. There is a surplus of indignation, and that surplus expresses itself in a sense of betrayal. Nor is it a sense of personal betrayal, as when someone you know lets you down. Rather, it is a sense that impersonal standards that we were somehow implicitly counting on have been deeply violated. What scandalizes us is not just some miscalculation or expected payoff we did not receive. We expected much more than someone dancing as close as possible to the line of misconduct without crossing it. Rather, it is as if something that we expected to be upheld—something well beyond the idea "I might get caught"—had not entered into our leaders' thinking and subsequent behavior.

So the story I have been telling about performance-based distrust is more positive than it might first appear. Even the scoundrel who is trying to deceive us by using "good" reasons to hide his "real" reasons is conveying something positive about the expected ethical sensibilities that are involved. In a backhanded way, our capacity to feel betrayed speaks to a residual trust in institutional values. Without holding this deeper, usually unarticulated presupposition, we might feel annoyed or bemused but not scandalized. In other words, the performance we care about is not simply a matter of leaders failing to "deliver the goods." In a larger sense, it is a matter of their failing to deliver the Good that was rightly expected of someone in an institutionally responsible position.

Culture-Based Distrust

We began this chapter with an account of the widespread cynicism directed toward institutions that has come to characterize our times. Noting that this is odd given what seems a human disposition toward rootedness, we went on to discuss at some length how this distrust of institutions has been both earned and magnified during the past half-century.

One is tempted to leave it at that and not broach the troublesome issue of culture, which is often used as an escape hatch to explain anything and everything. However, if we content ourselves with a strictly performance-based explanation of institutional distrust, something much too important is going to be left out of the picture. What we would be missing is the dominant view that we moderns hold regarding our moral position in the world. That sounds rather grand, but it is really saying nothing more than this: in contemporary society there has come to be a widely shared view of how people ought to get on with life. This outlook is not developed systematically enough to be called a moral philosophy, but it surely is pervasive enough to be called a cultural norm. And it helps greatly in accounting for our contemporary distrust of institutions.

In the next chapter we will have more to say about why it has become so difficult to put ourselves into a mind-set for thinking institutionally. For now the point is to get clear on the connection between our modern moral outlook and our general distrust of institutions.

Do I really dare claim that in a society as large and complex as ours there is a pervasive cultural norm about how people should get on with their lives? All sorts of divisions and controversies in our society will immediately come to mind. Isn't contemporary society supposed to be suffering from an uncentered, postmodern angst where there is no fixed or shared meaning? As a matter of fact there can be a great many divisions and ambiguities even while people's thinking is still wheeling around a pivotal point. Our "modernity" does not prevent there being such a cultural centerpiece. If anything, we can invoke a collective noun such as modernity and find it at least halfway intelligible precisely because there is such a moral centerpiece. Once it is put into words, I think you will immediately recognize the sway it holds.

Our moral polestar amounts to this central idea: the correct way to get on with life is to recognize that each of us has the right to live as he or she pleases so long as we do not interfere with the right of other people to do likewise.

Most people reading that statement will probably find it a bland truism, and, of course, the fact that we should find it so is precisely the point. Whether it is called the doctrine of live and let live, or our national creed's equal right to the pursuit of happiness, or just the American Dream, it dominates our thinking. We are each entitled to frame and live out a plan of life to suit ourselves so long as our actions or inactions do not harm others. That is our affirmation. We might recall from reading John Stuart Mill's *On Liberty* that the same principle can be inverted into a protective prohibition. When is compulsion (either through legal punishment or moral coercion) against individual liberty justified? The answer comes back that the only legitimate reason for any government, social group, or other person to interfere with my individual liberty is for the protection of other people.

As a guiding principle there is a lovely internal balance to it, a gyroscopic equilibrium that has undoubtedly been of great help in creating an individually energetic as well as collectively ordered society. One motion imparts the drive to hosts of individuals convinced that they are free to choose their own life projects independent of the likes or dislikes of anyone else. A second motion calibrates limits whereby we acknowledge the rights and interests of others. So, at least in principle, we arrive at that dynamic balance of individuality, liberty, tolerance, and regard for others that marks a genuinely democratic society.

If that sounds familiar it is because it has been the dominant moral framework taught in our public schools for roughly the past century. At the beginning of that period, George Bernard Shaw claimed that in modern progressive society the Golden Rule is that there is no Golden Rule. This clever turn of phrase risked turning the corner into nihilism, and John Dewey as well as others in the reform movement for progressive education would have none of that. Instead, generations of students were taught something like a semi-Golden Rule, prescribing that, short of harming others, every person should be free to seek out his or her own Golden Rule without being judged or casting judgments on others.

To be sure, there is a glitch in the argument. If there is to be no telling other people how to live, how does one get away with telling other people to live by that precept?

The way around that in the schools has been to invoke the vision of a larger democratic faith. In this view, democracy is an ongoing, experimental inquiry into ways of solving public problems. It requires citizens with a similar, open, tolerant quality of intelligence who, like the democratic system as a whole, are engaged in a continuous creative process of self-realization. Society becomes more democratic as individuals become more equal in their freedom to seek out and choose the personal meanings for their lives. What is good for the individual and good for democracy become the same thing. Thus the ideal, endorsed in the classroom and the culture, is a society of free individuals making self-validating choices that respect, without judging, the equal freedom of others.

Although it developed over many decades, this cultural model of the liberated, morally concerned but nonjudgmental individual was brought to the fore by the dramatic upheavals of the 1960s (which in cultural terms covered roughly the years 1955–1975). The transformative impact of this period is now the subject of a large scholarly literature, and I will not presume to describe it here. One of the best brief statements about what happened was given by the polling expert Daniel Yankelovich writing in 1981:

> Throughout most of this century, Americans believed that self-denial made sense, sacrificing made sense, obeying the rules made sense, subordinating the self to the institution made sense. But doubts have now set in, and Americans now believe that the old giving/getting compact needlessly restricts the individual while advancing the power of large institutions—government and business particularly—who use the power to enhance their own interests at the expense of the public.[18]

It takes one short step to connect this dominant cultural norm to an explanation for our widespread distrust of institutions. Whatever else might be said about them, all institutions present themselves as authoritative rules for behavior. To say that some structure, process, or precedent has become institutionalized means, at a minimum, that there is now a way of doing things to which people are expected to conform. Likewise, when we describe something as becoming deinstitutionalized we are saying, at a minimum, that the old rules of the game no longer appear to apply. The expectations of proper performance are dissolving.

Modern thinking inherently distrusts institutions because they are barriers and weights that impede our personal journeys toward meaning. The semi-Golden Rule tends to overrule what is most institutional about institutions. Our right to live as we please is at odds with any deference to an external authority or inherited ways in governing our lives. The heroic journey of self-discovery requires liberation from institutions' preexisting claims for respect, restraint, and obedience. Authentic individuality demands a free and tolerant exploration of personal choices, but institutions demand that we judge these choices, our own and everyone else's. Thus it seems that for us to grow into intelligent, independent adults, institutions are the home we must leave.

All of this casts institutions in a negative light, to say the least. Of course, we moderns can still be found acknowledging our support for various institutional arrangements, such as the legal system, private property, a particular sports tradition, perhaps even marriage. We are rightly concerned about an "authentic" individuality. And in that cause modern people can freely choose to make commitments that are institutional in nature. Indeed, a good part of this book is devoted to urging that we become more self-conscious about and learn to value precisely such commitments.

Nonetheless, there is no escaping a brute fact. In making any such institutional commitment, we are working against the grain of our contemporary culture. Having a modern outlook, we know that even at their best, institutions restrict our liberty and at their worst simply oppress people. Institutions are about chains. Jean Jacques Rousseau was an early master in the modern journey of self-expression and put the point this way: *"Civil man is born, lives, and dies in slavery. At his birth he is sewed in swaddling clothes; at his death he is nailed in a coffin. So long as he keeps his human shape, he is enchained by our institutions."*[19]

Rousseau could not have imagined the dense world of massive institutional structures that even the most isolated citizen inhabits today. The change from a traditional to a modern society shifted governing relationships away from face-to-face status bonds to contract-based exchanges, and then to ever more impersonal bureaucratic dependencies. I do not think one has to be a Marxist to appreciate the sense of alienation that can come with experiencing this modern world. Maneuvering daily among the massive structures of modern economic, political, and social power, we are often reminded that we are not living the lives we would have chosen. By the mid-twentieth century, observers from the political left, right, and center were describing this sense of alienation—the self-estrangement of "growing up absurd" to become an "organization man" in the "lonely crowd." Whether or not one subscribes to C. Wright Mills's theory of a power elite, the opening paragraph of his 1956 book is an apt characterization:

> The powers of ordinary men are circumscribed by the everyday worlds in which they live, yet even in these rounds of job, family, and neighborhood they often seem driven by forces they can neither understand nor govern. "Great changes" are beyond their control, but affect their conduct and outlook none the less. The very framework of modern society confines them to projects not their own, but from every side, such changes now press upon the men and women of the mass society, who accordingly feel that they are without purpose in an epoch in which they are without power.[20]

To live in our times is to be thoroughly dependent on the competence and dutifulness of strangers in far-flung institutional settings, people with whom we have never contracted, much less really know. Institutions can evoke our distrust because we need them so much. Resentment is the price self-respect extracts for such dependence. Although the realities of daily life keep us from living up to its ideal, the autonomy we cherish is what makes the semi-Golden Rule shine so golden for us. Thus we moderns have a culture-based distrust of institutions both because they get in our way and also because we cannot get out of their way. In the modern mental landscape, institutional distrust goes with the territory.

And yet, as with performance-based distrust, implicit in the preceding discussion there is a redeeming counterpoint that serves to endorse institutional values. Once you think about it, any thoroughgoing "culture-based distrust" of institutions is an unsustainable absurdity. Human beings simply cannot and do not live that way.

In the next chapter I will have much more to say about different ways of conceptualizing and defining the term "institution." Without trying to justify it here, let me simply observe that institutions represent inheritances of valued purpose with attendant rules and moral obligations. They constitute socially ordered grounding for human life. This grounding in a normative field implicates the lives of individuals and collectivities in a lived-out social reality. To live in a culture that turns its back on institutions is equivalent to trying to live in a physical body without its skeleton or hoping to use a language but not its grammar. A culture wholly committed to distrusting its institutions is a self-contradiction.

To be sure, there are more than enough contradictions in our modern way of life to keep social critics in full-time employment. However, there are also what must be trillions of daily transactions in our society that amount to constant microendorsements of institutional values. As we noted earlier, these occur as people simply get on with the ordinary business of daily living. And there are good reasons why ordinary life, even in our modern society, should have some institution-affirming qualities.

To see why that is so it is helpful to recall what it means to say we trust or distrust. What it means is not that we are simply registering a feeling. Trust is an action verb. To trust or distrust entails behavioral enactments that are nicely captured in various ways by the Hebrew language—to lean on, or take refuge in, or wait for, or lay full confidence on somebody or something. It turns out that taking this sort of action is inescapable in daily life, and it often brings us to count on what is authoritative and enduring—in other words, institutional—in nature. There are at least three reasons why "the affirmation of ordinary life" keeps pushing us in the direction of affirming institutional values. Because the reasons are indeed ordinary, it can take a special effort to notice them.

In the first place, there is an immense psychological bu
that comes with the freedom to seek out and choose what
personal meanings our lives are to have. The more seriously we
take this right to live as we please, the greater the burden. That
is because it requires that we must get all the truth and meaning of things for ourselves, or else go without it. Pushing tradition and every other external authority to the side and relying
on ourselves alone is a heroic stance toward the world in literary fiction and popular songs. But in real life it is likely to be a
recipe, not for freedom, but for continuous confusion, anxiety,
and dread. Because of that, people often prefer to forget the
wealth of possibilities open to them. Moreover, to set choice as
your ultimate value on this journey of self-discovery leaves
everything you are doing with an inevitable weightlessness.
Admiring choice for its own sake is tantamount to saying that
it really does not matter what you choose. It is actually to
admire nothing. If the most important thing is that I run my life
as I choose, then any larger meaning to what I am doing evap-
orates in a sea of willfulness. Everything else about my life that
might have significance is thinned out into the process of
choosing. And when I have made my last choice, perhaps dis-
abled, aged, or just frustrated with all the choosing, nothing else
about me will matter either.

The result of this psychological reality is that in our daily
lives the semi-Golden Rule does not leave us in the free, liberated condition that it seemed to promise. It leaves us perplexed,
burdened, and looking for some fixed points of reference. To disparage this turning to reference points as a weak-willed attempt
to "escape from freedom" is to overlook the fact that we all must
bring the myriad of choices we face into some manageable and
meaningful form. To be manageable implies choosing less than
everything potentially available for choice, and to be meaningful implies choices weighted with a larger significance than the
empty fact that we happen to have made them.

In the second place, even if we could bear the psychological burden, the fact of the matter is that our everyday actions

inevitably end up being grounded in at least some institutional reference points. To escape from relying on authority is a practical impossibility as we work our way through daily life.

To see why that is so, we need to avoid the modern conceit of thinking that "authority" means the same thing as "authoritarian." Stripped of its modern ideological baggage, the concept of authority concerns, not what is authoritarian, but what is authorial. From its Latin sources, it means one who bears witness to the authenticity of something, such as a legal document. For example, that is what Augustine means when he says that "in practical life" we owe our beliefs to authority. To illustrate this, he goes back to the most elemental of everyday human relationships. If we refuse to believe what we have not proven for ourselves, how can a person feel any duty to his parents? I have to take it on the authority of my mother as to who my father is. But she in turn may be deceived that she is my mother, unless she takes it on the authority of midwives and servants that babies were not switched at delivery. As Augustine concludes, "Nothing at all of human society remains safe, if we shall determine to believe nothing, which we cannot grasp by full apprehension."[21] The modern assumption is that limiting options limits our humanity. But every action we take is a selection and exclusion. To choose anything is also to reject what was not chosen. Just as the only way to keep all your options open is never to choose anything, the only way to be fully free is never to act.

It is as a matter of sheer practicality that we refuse to leave ourselves isolated in such a sea of willful confusion. We do not go back to first principles and reason out our own complete philosophy for each decision we find ourselves required to make. Otherwise, on any given day we would never make the first foray out of our bedroom. What we typically go back to and "lean on" are the experiences and forms accumulated, not by us personally, but by the collaboration of multiple generations. To get on with life, we repeatedly entrust ourselves to the knowledge others have acquired and bear witness to. So as we live out answers to the inescapable question of "whom/what do you trust, or distrust

least?" we end up counting on what seems enduring and authoritative. Such practicality in ordinary life pushes us toward the
implicit endorsement of institutional values.

A final qualification to culture-based distrust centers on our
inherent social needs as human beings. These are indeed considerations that move us every day. The need begins on our very
first day, because women's pelvic structure is such that we are the
only mammals that need the help of others to deliver offspring.[22] Living out our family lives, we do not want to think
that other family members are constantly mulling over the
choice of whether or not to care for and be committed to each
other. Should we fall into the hands of doctors, teachers, or
policemen, we do not want to have to wonder if this happens to
be a day when they have chosen to fulfill their professional
responsibilities rather than a day when they have decided to
reject those external constraints on their liberty. We want the
fiduciary relationships of institutions to matter because for our
own good we need them to matter.

Even in our mundane interactions with strangers, we
depend on a basic, institutionalized trust that makes meaningful
human interactions possible. To transform our ambiguous utter-
ances into a "normal" conversation is a remarkable practical
accomplishment. It depends on our tacit acceptance of common
social knowledge and expectations, as well as our willingness to
do the accommodative work that keeps our conversation meaningful. As an early critic of the modern complexities of life
observed, "When one must first question words and intentions,
and start from the premise that everything said and written is
meant to offer us an illusion in place of truth, life becomes
strangely complicated."[23] It does indeed (hence the devastating
consequences of the *PR effect* discussed earlier).

To say with Aristotle that man is a political animal is saying
far too little. Man alone expresses the nature of his political and
social attachments through institutions rather than mere
instincts. To take one example of a social relationship with
strangers, it is an absolutely extraordinary thing to institutional-

ize in law the idea of "innocent until proven guilty." As the late president of Yale, Kingman Brewster, observed: "The presumption of innocence is not just a legal concept. In commonplace terms it rests on that generosity of spirit which assumes the best, not the worst, in the stranger."[24] Having this presumption embedded in our law and society helps us live in a world where, as strangers to each other, you and I are more likely to be regarded as a potential friend than an enemy. It is a remarkable, institutionalized way of supporting some part of our human need for social attachments. However, to notice such things we must be willing to pay deliberate attention rather than drift past the glories of everyday life.

★ ★ ★

I have tried to indicate the psychological burden, the simple practicality, and the human need that together help drive us toward the affirmation of institutional values in our daily business of getting on with life. These three forces are not separate but are woven into the fabric of living out each day. The psychological burden of enacting our ideal of personal autonomy is not consciously calculated and laid aside. Its diffuse anxiety is simply sidestepped as we follow the semiautomatic routines and practical understandings of daily life. And these in turn work in manifold, usually unnoticed ways, to meet many of our human needs.

So let us end by returning to Rousseau and those swaddling clothes. My point is not that it is wrong to see that institutions can be cages of oppression. My point is that this is a dangerously incomplete half-truth. Institutions can also be a home-place of reference for enriched, flourishing lives. Rousseau got it badly wrong. What he depicted as "enchaining" were in fact signs of human nurturing. The swaddling clothes and coffins are giving witness. They are institutionalized testimony to the belief that human beings are born as something more than beasts dropped in a field, and that they die as something more than animals left dead on the roadside. To be sure, institutions are constraints on any absolute license to do whatever we want, but they can be *enabling* constraints that make it possible for us to live out and further develop our humanity.

Here then is the impasse we are having to endure in these times. It is a stalemate between the distrust that various institutions have richly earned and the vague appreciation of institutional values that makes possible our sense of betrayal when that has happened. Likewise, it is a stalemate between our cultural norm of individual autonomy free from the demands of external authority, and the inescapable need to entrust ourselves to some such authority. We will not and cannot go back to a simpler time when deference to institutional authority was usually taken for granted. And in our worldly savvy, we see no way of going forward to a brighter, saner world of trust. We are like the inhabitants of Limbo in Dante's *Inferno.* Of them it has been said, "Their failure lay in not imagining better."[25] But what would it mean to "imagine better" when it comes to our view of institutions?

CHAPTER THREE
FROM THINKING ABOUT INSTITUTIONS TO THINKING INSTITUTIONALLY

I believe it is possible to imagine being both thoroughly modern and more deeply committed to institutional values. By thoroughly modern I mean that we will probably continue to be distrustful of institutions and on guard against their power over us. And rightfully so, given the harm they can do to us. However, I also think that we can achieve a saner way of life by more self-consciously learning how to think and act institutionally. Along with a prudent regard for institutional failings, a turning of thought and action toward institutional values could also prevent much harm and do us great good.

That combination of views—to distrust but value—gives my answer to the question left hanging at the end of the last chapter. To spell out what "imagining better" might mean is the purpose of this chapter. Not for a moment would I presume to claim that I am offering a cure-all for our modern impasse. However, I do think that this notion of "distrust but value" can help guide us through a good many perplexities of our modern plight. To repeat, that plight is the legitimate distrust of and inescapable need for institutions that we feel in our lives.

We will begin by reviewing the problem of defining institutions and then consider five major ways in which social scientists have tried to think about this subject. The aim is to distill some themes from this scholarship that can be helpful in organizing one's thinking on the subject. Combining insights from the different schools will help to clarify how institutions are related to our view of individual preferences, historical change, and organizational values. From there, considering the meaning of rational calculation will begin to take us beyond the boundaries of the existing schools as the issues of institutional purpose and morality come into view.

Obviously these are huge subjects that would exhaust us long before we could ever exhaust them. Here, the best I can hope for is to expose some essential themes, or as the legal scholar Karl Llewellyn once put it, "to talk sense in rugged outline."

A World of Institutions (and Scholarly Disagreement)

Given the risk of sinking into a morass of purely academic distinctions, I have so far diligently avoided defining the term "institution." The time has come to take that risk. It is worth reviewing the ways in which social scientists have been thinking about institutions because this provides a good platform for moving to a different perspective on the subject (which we will then begin to do toward the end of this chapter). And to advocate taking that step is really the point of this book.

Unfortunately, as far as definitions go, reviews of the scholarly literature on institutions are an invitation to frustration. The reviewers generally make a point of describing how the leading experts on the subject simply cannot agree on what constitutes an institution.[1] From this, the unhappy reader might conclude that for all their efforts, these highly credentialed thinkers really cannot tell you what they are thinking about. More charitably, what one learns is that there are different schools of thought about the meaning of institutions. In fact, working through the types of definitions amounts to generating a survey of the major theoretical approaches that constitute modern social science. Some of these schools overlap in places, some are diametrically opposed, and some simply talk past each other—so much so that anyone trying to make sense of it all might be tempted to despair. But amid all the apparent confusion about defining an institution, there really are some important things that can be learned concerning how people think about institutions. Working our way through the array of conceptualizations takes some effort, but in the end I think it is worthwhile.

For those critical of my earlier dereliction of definitional duties, Box 3.1 more than adequately overcompensates, with twenty-one definitions of the term "institution." I have selected this range of definitions from the work of leading social scientists, and well over a hundred other entries could easily have been added to the pool. It is an especially rich pool because of the renewed attention that was directed toward the meaning of the concept in the last quarter of the twentieth century. That was a time when academic interest in a "new institutionalism" swept through the various social science disciplines. The result is a far larger and more variegated list of definitions than could have been compiled only a few decades prior. Alas, the world of institutions includes a world of disputations concerning how to think about institutions.

One strategy for dealing with this daunting complexity would be to try to extract what seems common among all of the definitions. Such a search for the one or more elements that all things designated as an institution must share is called an essentialist definition. A quick look at Box 3.1 shows that many, if not most, experts seem to agree that institutions have to do with creating and enforcing rules.

Fair enough. But once we start looking into this "essence," it turns out that scholars reviewing this subject find that here too there is significant disagreement about the definition of the term "rule." For example, the philosopher John Rawls pointed out

Box 3.1 An Institution Is...

1. the body of laws that establish the set of rights and obligations in force.

2. a formal governmental organization defined by public laws.

3. the formal rules and procedures established by the action of governments and backed by the coercive power of the state.

4. a designed and formalized structure that increases rulers' bargaining power, reduces their transaction costs, and lowers their discount rates so as to allow rulers better to capture gains from political exchanges.

5. a system of rules governing actions in pursuit of immediate ends in terms of their conformity with the ultimate common value system of the community. An institution is a complex of integrated roles of strategic structural significance in the social system whereby action-expectations are integrated with the value patterns governing in society.

6. the basic focus of social organization regulating the perennial problems of any society (reproduction, socialization, production, distribution, and the like) through definite and continuous patterns that are upheld by norms and their sanctions.

7. a settled habit of thought common to the generality of men tied to the community's status system and verified by such authority as custom, law, politics, religion, and morality.

8. a largely unplanned product (a group or practice) of social adaptation that expresses a stable, integrative pattern in the fabric of social life. The social entanglements and commitments of institutions are recognized as more than purely instrumental and infused with value beyond the technical requirements of the task at hand. As socialization aims at giving moral shape to individuals, institutionalization seeks to realize moral values in the world of collective social groups and practices.

9. a way of thought or action of some prevalence and permanence that is embedded in the habits of a group or the customs of a people. Institution is the singular of which the mores and folkways are the plural. It constitutes the standards of conformity from which an individual may depart only at his peril.

10. a set of rules (for example, roles, procedures, offices) that emerges from and subsequently structures human interactions. Institutions are persistent means of coordinating social, economic, and political interactions and thus represent large-scale coordination equilibria.

11. the organized administrative capacities of the state as they develop through time.

12. a rule structure designed under particular historical circumstances. Institutions shape pathways for the subsequent development of ideas, interests, and interactions among state and societal actors.

13. a game form laying down rules defining eligible participants, permissible modes of deliberation, prospective outcomes, and the manner in which players' preferences are to be revealed.

14. the rules of the game in a society or, more generally, the humanly devised constraints for structuring human interaction. Institutions are made up of formal constraints (rules, laws, constitutions), informal constraints (norms of behavior, conventions, and so forth), and their enforcement characteristics. Together they define the incentive structure of societies.

15. a set of interpersonal rules about behavior, especially about making decisions.

16. a set of rules that evolve or emerge from the repetitive play of an underlying game by a group of rational actors/agents.

17. an equilibrium way of doing things. Strictly speaking, there is no separate entity that we can identify as an institution. There is only rational behavior, conditioned on expectations about the behavior and reactions of others. When these expectations take on a particularly clear form across individuals, apply to situations recurring over a long time, and especially when they involve highly variegated and specific expectations about the different roles of different actors in determining what actions others should take, we often collect these expectations and strategies under the heading institution.

18. a macro-level abstraction in which cognitions are shared in defining what has meaning and what actions are possible. The institution is made up of taken-for-granted scripts, rules, and classifications. Rationalized and impersonal prescriptions are shared "typifications" independent of any particular entity to which moral allegiance might be owed.

19. a socially-constructed, routine-reproducing program or rule system. Institutions operate as relative fixtures of constraining environments and are accompanied by taken-for-granted accounts. They represent a self-activating reproduction process in that they do not require repeated mobilization and active interventions in order to operate.

20. a symbolic system with nonobservable, absolute, transrational referents constituting the institution's particular central logic and observable social relations making that logic concrete. Through these concrete social relations, individuals and organizations strive to achieve their ends, but they also make life meaningful and reproduce those symbolic systems. The routines of each institution are connected to rituals that define the order of the world and one's position within it.

21. a convention arising from a common interest that ensures cooperation, but a convention that is also intrinsically not merely instrumentally valued. It is regarded as possessing a self-validating truth analogous to the natural order.[2]

that rules can be portrayed as summaries of past decisions that allow the observer to predict future behavior. In that case, participants can change the rules as they choose without engaging in self-contradictory behavior (for example, as a rule, Americans have vacationed in the summertime, and now they are deciding to take shorter holidays throughout the year). But alongside the "summary view" of rules, there is also the "practice conception" of rules. In this conception, being taught how to engage in a practice involves being instructed in the rules that define the practice and appealing to those rules to correct the behavior of those engaged in it. Here, engaging in the practice while chang–

ing the rules is self-contradictory (for example, our soccer team's improved greatly once we abandoned that rule about not touching the ball with your hands).[3]

As if that were not enough, it turns out that the meaning of the word "definition" is itself thoroughly contested. The experts tell us that "there are few if any philosophical questions about definition . . . on which logicians and philosophers agree."[4] Going back to the list of definitions in Box 3.1, we can find the meaning of institutions being conceptualized by *genealogy* (where they come from), or *function* (what they do), or *purpose* (what they are meant for), and/or *essence* (what they are). Some of the definitions we read are *explanatory* (seeking to clarify important aspects of a concept). Others are *analytic* (specifying the type of thing the term applies to and the differences from other things of the same type). Or we might resort to metaphorical examples of the term, as in saying that institutions are "history encoded into rules," or "frozen decisions," or "congealed tastes."[5] And perhaps at the end of the day we might want to capitulate and say that "institution" is a basic, elemental concept which cannot be defined (except through synonyms, which means word substitutions that are no definition at all). The philosopher Martin Buber observed that man's twofold attitude accords with the two basic words man can speak: the irreducible word pairs, I-You and I-It. Likewise, some people might say that in trying to fathom our social existence we must give up on definition and accept "institution" as the irreducible word pair I-We.

Although it is frustrating to find that there is no agreed definition of the term "institution," that does not have to prevent us from moving forward to clarify the ways of thinking about the concept. Since the days of the ancient Greeks, philosophers have experienced the same frustration in trying to find the unchanging essences of things in this world of ever-changing sense phenomena. And in our own scientific age we are still left wondering about the meaning of primary terms. For example, if we ask what is energy, the likely answer will be that it is the ability to do work. But that tells us what energy does, not what it is. We naturally think that energy has to *be* something before it can *do* something, so we are left wondering what is the "it" that can do work.

A way around this problem is to look at concepts such as institution in a different way (sometimes called a polythetic definition). This view does not require that all institutions have one or more specific elements in common. Instead of seeking the essential feature(s), we can make more progress by identifying family resemblances among the things generally thought of as institutions. That is a helpful approach because in calling something an institution, all we have to agree on are general traits that exist to a greater or lesser degree. We do not have to claim to have found the common denominator among all institutions.[6] Things are what they are, but they can be more or less of what they are.

When we look over Box 3.1 in this frame of mind, there are discernible clusters that do identify something like family traits. I admit to having stacked the deck a little, because you will see that the definitions are presented in those clusters of family traits. There might be a few weird cousins, but I think that they are recognizable as belonging to one particular family lineage and not another. Reviewing the definitions offered in Box 3.1, it would be wrong to conclude that they are saying basically the same thing (and assuredly there are strenuous arguments over the perceived differences).

However, it would also be wrong to conclude that these definitions are all totally different in their understanding of institutions. In pondering Box 3.1, what we find are shared differences that point us toward various schools of thought. These intellectual leanings in thinking about institutions can be arranged into five categories, although there certainly are other reasonable divisions that might be used.[7] These are presented in the rough sequence with which they appeared on the social science scene over the last hundred years. In parentheses I have indicated relevant definitions from Box 3.1 and a major work centered in (though the authors are too intelligent to be wholly contained within) each school.

The Statist School

Long before legal and political science disciplines were distinguished from each other, institutions were the focal point of study in what some called the science of the state. In that view the basic units of institutional analysis are legally constituted structures (rather than, say, contracting individuals or socially embedded roles). Our attention is drawn to formal governmental organizations, legal processes, and systems of law (rather than social context or informal practices). Such institutions make up the forms of government, and they express authoritative power relationships (rather than, for example, cooperative exchanges). There is room for conscious design in institutions, especially in legal codes and constitutions. However, the emphasis is on historical evolution, in the sense that legal and political instrumentalities emerge organically in the building and operating of the state.[8]

The Social Systems School

Emile Durkheim famously declared sociology to be the science of institutions, and ever since many social scientists have sought to think about institutions in light of the workings, not of the state, but of the macrolevel social system. Usually this has occurred through a functional analysis whereby institutions serve to integrate individual behavior into the performance of various social functions or, more generally, the realization of community values. Institutions are seen to do this through socially constructed roles that are coupled with cultural norms, conventions, and status structures to govern expected behavior within and across roles. Formal organizations and laws are part of this picture of integrative human association but, like individuals, are embedded and shot through with informal societal influences. Any idea of institutions as designed or chosen is subordinated to notions of unplanned patterns of social adaptation and the functionality of institutions for system maintenance.[9]

The Historical-Institutionalist School

Operating at the intersection of political science and history disciplines, the historical analysis of institutions has some roots in the statist school. However, it was eclipsed for several decades after World War II by a concern in the social sciences to give preference to "behavioral realities" over institutional forms. With challenges to the stability of Western democratic regimes in the 1960s and 1970s and subsequent pressures of globalization, there has been a renewed emphasis on the semiautonomous institutions of the state. However, unlike the statists, this school's focus is on political institutions in interaction with social groups and movements, especially the evolutionary development of these relationships through time. Institutions organize and apply the authoritative decision-making power of the state.

But they do so as time-factored phenomena. Often created in response to some crisis, institutions preserve stability by adapting to changing circumstances of their social setting, thereby to a greater or lesser extent acquiring value, legitimacy, and predictability (institutionalization). However, institutions' creation and adaptations in turn affect the later contours of that sociopolitical setting. Past choices—creating a new policy, administrative structure, or intellectual approach—carry a cumulative weight into the future, shaping actors' routines, expectations, and allowable preferences. Thus a pathway is put in place for subsequent state-society interactions to be elaborated and evolve.[10]

The Rational Choice School

Using the standard model from economics, this school builds on the assumption of instrumentally rational actors in pursuit of their individual self-interests. Rather than pushed from behind by inertial forces of social norms or guided along pathways of historical–political contingency, the inhabitants of this world are pulled forward by calculation of future outcomes to maximize their individual utilities. Individuals pursue their given preferences through voluntary exchanges that, unfortunately, are encumbered by contractual and other procedural problems (hence the centrality of rules rather than organizations in this school). Institutions are the procedural rules used by such rational individuals to solve problems of opportunism, imperfect information, costly monitoring, and enforcement.

These rules of the game may be externally imposed constraints on the players, or they may be equilibrium conditions produced by rules the players themselves design and choose. In either case, institutions allow gains from exchange, which would otherwise be lost, to be realized in the aggregation of individual preferences. Thus, in place of functionalism at the macrolevel presented in the sociologists' school, the rational choice school offers a functionalism at the microlevel, where institutions serve the interests of individual utility maximizers.[11]

The Cognitive School

Various strands of psychology, cultural analysis, and organizational theory in sociology can be usefully considered together because of their focus on the cognitive processes underlying institutions. Here the appropriate model of behavior is not individual choice and calculation but socially constructed patterns of thought. Hence the "interpretivist" character of this school. Uncertainty and limitations in human rationality are coped with by organizational routines, habits of allocating attention, ready-made narratives, and other mental templates. Decision-making is more often about rule following than about the calculation of consequences. Institutions are the sedimented deposits of such taken-for-granted accounts, classifications, performance scripts, rationalized myths, and other shared "typifications."

The important thing is that these ready-made accounts, although socially constructed, become accepted as objective reality exterior to the person—which is to say, they become institutions. The inherited institutional frames of language and symbols establish approved means and define desired outcomes for action. By conventions of appropriateness certain actions are associated with certain situations. Hence institutions do not just constrain options; they also establish the very criteria by which people discover their preferences. Institutions evolve slowly and inefficiently because individuals cannot often conceive of unscripted alternatives.[12]

★ ★ ★

From this little survey, we can reasonably conclude that it matters whether one is talking about a legal institution, social institution, economic institution, political institution, or cultural institution. But it matters much more whether it is a lawyer, sociologist, economist, political scientist, or psychologist who is doing the talking. Depending on your school of thought, institutions are consciously designed and chosen. Or they are unintended by-products of power struggles and other social interactions. Or they emerge organically with the norms and values produced by the logic of their own functioning. And again, depending on your way of thinking about them, institutions are structures for the exercise of power, or they are means of facilitating individuals' mutually beneficial cooperation, or they are adaptive instrumentalities of social learning over time. Institutions are rules for human interaction, or they are structures for enforcing rules, or they are the behavioral regularities produced by the rules. If taken strictly on their own terms, the five schools can leave us in an even worse quandary than the search for the essentialist definition when it comes to thinking about institutions.

Fortunately, borders between the various schools are unenforceable, and scholars can move around quite freely if they are so inclined. Such disciplinary trespassing makes sense for thinking about something as complex and pervasive as institutions.

Analysis takes things apart, often to great intellectual advantage. The problem, of course, is that in order to make sense of human affairs we also have to keep trying to put back together what analysis has taken apart. So it is with the various schools for thinking about institutions. Their analytic sharpness, which can seem irresistible in the classroom, is under constant threat from the yearning to "get real," which typically means seeking a more integrated or at least balanced perspective.

Identifying the schools and their definitions is worth doing because it helps us, first, to appreciate the insights of each group, and second, to understand the thinking beyond which we are likely to need to move. Blended thinking, rather than dogmatic school loyalty, often produces more insight. Thus it is not unreasonable to expect that institutions may well contain, in varying degrees, the designed and the organic, human intentions and accidental social by-products accumulated from the past. Likewise we are likely to understand more of the real world if we remain open to the idea that institutions are about things structured and formally organized, and that they are also about things unstructured and implicit. For example, any rounded analysis will want to know about the institution of the contract and its surrounding legal apparatus, and it will just as surely want to know about the institution of the handshake and its surrounding cultural understandings that make the writing of contracts feasible.

Thinking along the same lines, we can understand that, by freeing up people for action within constraints, institutions can be simultaneously vehicles of control and of empowerment. The duality is analogous to an early engineering problem in automobiles. Engines making cars ever faster could be designed, but they were of no use to people until adequate braking systems were invented.[13] All accelerator doesn't work, and all brake doesn't work. The brake/accelerator combination allows freedom of movement.

Blended thinking across the schools is not the same thing as sloppy eclecticism. It is not saying that anything goes. It is saying that there is probably more to be gained by combining and exploiting the various schools' insights than by adhering slavishly to their scripts. Within the confines of any one school it is easy to end up with an undersocialized or an oversocialized, an underhistoricized or an overhistoricized view of human action. Human attempts at purposive action are situated in contexts of social relations, cultural understandings, and historical pathways. At the same time, we are dealing with creatures—rational actors, if you like—who are not automatons. With an inherent capacity for calculative action, they are agents and not just the objects of society, culture, and history. How loose or tight the hold of such contextual forces might be is a matter for investigation, not a priori conclusions. Being manifold, human action resists scholars' intellectual boxes.

Experienced practitioners in the various schools understand this and often seek out richer forms of combinatorial thinking about institutions. They try to build on particular insights that different schools might offer on the fascinating and truly wonderful thing that is man's ongoing social experience. We can consider examples of such hybrid thinking in light of three vexing problems in institutional analysis: (1) individual preferences, (2) historic change, and (3) organizational values.

1. Rational individuals may be seeking to satisfy their preferences, but where do they get their preferences? In the economic marketplace, self-interest may be largely self-defining (as in buy low, sell high). But schools 2, 3, and 5 insist on the larger point that people defining their interests and objectives are situated in social, historical, and political contexts. Rational choice theorists know this, but they also know that it can be analytically useful to assume that preferences are held in a fixed, predetermined way by rational individuals. Treating that as a provisional assumption (rather than a truth claim about the universal human condition), they can develop analytic models that may help to clarify underlying relationships.

But leading rational choice theorists have also recognized the need to fill in and stretch these frameworks with empirical material. And that means trying to understand what it is that actors are seeking to maximize *within* a given context of social, political, and cultural incentives. It also means being aware of how socially embedded norms, symbols, cultural scripts, and the like can shape strategic interactions. As something more than the formal rules of the "game," such contextual factors provide resources, signals, and focal points in those interactions, thus limiting the purely theoretical range of likely outcomes. Likewise, to help the contextualist schools' accounts from turning into an interpretive mush of unrelated details, some analytically disciplined models are needed.[14] The unsituated, rational individual and the socially embedded person are two important figures on the landscape. They need to be brought into a common narrative—and thoughtful members of the different schools know it.

2. Change is a major riddle in thinking about institutions. Surely one of the most common family traits of institutions is endurance. Institutions persist and preserve, or else they do not deserve the name. They exhibit stability, inertial force, lines of continuity stretching through time. All of this fits well with the statist school's view of a formal legal order, with the social system school's view of system maintenance functions, and with the rational choice school's view of equilibrium outcomes. On the other hand, institutions are clearly historical phenomena. They participate in the temporal nature of human existence. By what sort of mysterious quantum leap does one stable equilibrium order transition into another institutional order?

Scholars struggle with this question, but they struggle more successfully with it as they combine insights from the different schools. At any particular point in time institutions are indeed likely to be taken as givens. As such they are inertial, stabilizing forces—that is, they reflect and reinforce existing social relations, political distributions of power, cognitively taken-for-granted accounts, and the like. But to be enduring, institutions also have to be adaptive and change in time-factored ways. Do institutions weather time like rocks—solid, immovable, flaking at the margins? Or are they the crisis-induced replacements of one institutional order by another, a new set of china substituting for the set history has broken? Or is the time-factoring of institutions more organic, as they are reborn through time without having quite died, carrying on several overlapping lives?

Answers to these questions need not be mutually exclusive. If we are respectful of the insights from the different schools, it becomes clear that stability and change are not two separate questions. They are a single invitation to try to understand how each participates in the other—how stability is a source of change and change a source of stability.

For example, there certainly is an inert stability if institutions weather time as rocks do. But always to do the same thing as surrounding circumstances change is also, in a sense, not really to be doing the same thing. If my behavior stays the same as it was in college, while my friends go on to start families and develop their careers, what once looked like boyish charm will probably look more like childishness. So, too, when an institutionalized arrangement remains fixed in place while the relevant environment around it changes, this boulderlike fixedness can really amount to a transformative drift in the institution.[15] Nor should such a tendency be surprising. Institutions can be coordinating mechanisms, but they also express and continue to reinforce particular distributions of power that try to stay in place.

When change in the surrounding environment is sudden and deep (a war, major technological breakthrough, oil price shock, and the like), the very stability of long-established institutions may be a disadvantage and source of instability, especially as those invested in the institutions try to hold on to their privileged positions. At these critical junctures, an opening is created for those less rigidly bound by the rules of the game and power structures of the past. That is especially true for those groups and individuals heretofore disadvantaged by the status quo and biding their time to change it. In such crises, to say that one equilibrium order is being replaced by another really is not telling us very much. To understand the *change* that is under way we need to understand the *stability* that has existed—the varied interests and strategies of its supportive coalition, its opponents and their grievances, the methods that have renewed its support over time.[16] Whether dealing with individuals in your dorm room or institutional collectivities in society, to understand a breakdown it is important to know the preexisting condition that is breaking down. It is commonly observed that a seemingly stable status quo can contain seeds of its own destruction. But it is also true that there can be such things as seeds of nourishment in the status quo that help prevent destruction.

Crises and cases of "punctuated equilibrium" are only the most dramatic ways of encountering the interaction between change and stability. More subtle and common is the hidden drama of gradualism and cumulative patterns of change and stability. In the course of time, nothing can be more radical than an accumulation of many small, adjustive steps that no one notices. This is not to deny that there are critical junctures when institutional arrangements are overturned and reformulated. It is to say that we need to pay attention to how these outcomes are sustained, some becoming institutional legacies that are carried downstream rather than sunk in time's river.

Changes that reflect and reinforce the position of the powerful are obviously important for sustainability. But so too are more subtle adaptations. Accretion can gradually add new components to an institution's work. Accommodation to the perceived demands of the times can incrementally produce a redirection of institutional mission itself. The modern university is a good example. In the past one hundred years, the university's basic educational work on behalf of young adults has been enlarged to cover myriad research agendas, professional training, lucrative sports programs, combating racial and gender discrimination, government contracting, adult education, and on and on. At the same time a strong case can be made that in responding to the demands of business and student consumers, the university's basic mission—to prepare broadly educated citizens for life—has been redirected to training workers for the job market.

A broader view of the subject shows that institutions do not exist in isolation. Whether in critical times or more settled periods, the interplay of stability and change occurs across a population of institutions, each one emerging in its own time and foreshadowing the logic of its own pathway. Different institutions rest on different foundations of ideas, interests, and distributions of power. These multiple institutional orders at work in society interact with others through time, continually bringing new possibilities of both congruity and incongruity to the fore. Considered in isolation, each institutional arrangement may portray stability, but taken together their rebounding impacts on each other can repeatedly produce forces for change. Thus in thinking about institutions in an across-the-schools way, there need be no conflict between stasis and development.[17]

3. A final example of blending the insights from different schools concerns the connection between institutions and organizations. From the perspective of the statist school, to study institutions is essentially equivalent to studying formal organizations—namely, those organizations possessing the power of public authority. States are built by mobilizing human and material resources, by organizing those resources into effective structures for action, and by authoritatively enforcing on society the decisions of those structures. This perspective is important because, amid the welter of other, more nuanced ways of thinking about institutions, it keeps a central point in view. The state is not just one more "actor" on the historical stage. Its action is in the form of power, and its power is essentially monopolistic and coercive. The state may choose to persuade, bargain, or compromise for mutual advantage. But at the end of the day, those who control public authority have the final say in deciding who wins and who loses. And because it is the *public* authority speaking, those decisions apply to everybody, whether or not they were involved in making the decisions. Recalling this central point is essentially what the historical-institutionalist school has accomplished in "bringing the state back in."[18]

There is also a focus on institution-as-organization that takes a broader societal perspective. It does so under the general heading of bureaucratization, a systematic rationalization of human association that occurs and replicates itself throughout the public and private spheres of modern industrial society. Drawing on the insights of Max Weber, this sociological perspective pays attention to the thoroughgoing institutionalization of our lives, that being understood in terms of an inescapable participation in large-scale, special-purpose organizations making up the rational-legal order. These organizations are instruments rationally engineered to achieve specific goals through consciously coordinated activities (divisions of labor, trained expertise, impersonal rules, hierarchical chains of command, and the like). Historically observed, there is simply no denying that this does indeed constitute a central feature of what makes modern society modern as compared with preindustrial societies.

At the same time, the exaggerated claims of rationality (that would tend to merge concepts of institution, organization, and bureaucracy) have prompted valuable corrections from different perspectives. Within sociology, organization theory has found the rational model of organization to be unrealistic. The operative reality is that organizations are coalitions of shifting interest groups, negotiating goals with multiple, limited rationalities, accommodating themselves in anarchic ways to the stream of influences from their environments. Rather than rational instruments for achieving specific goals, organizational structure and behavior are driven by the need to survive. Organizations adapt to survival challenges in whatever ways will garner support and legitimacy. The cognitive school goes on to argue that to gain that support and legitimacy, formal organizational structures are shaped to reflect the myths of their institutional environment rather than the actual demands of their work activities. They project the appearance of rational organization because that is the script endorsed by the larger society. The rational choice school offers a similar critique, but in its own language. It explicitly accepts the idea of organizations and their inhabitants as rational actors, but contends that what they are being rational about is not the pursuit of professed public goals. Instead, their rationality is expressed in their self-interested pursuit of bureaucratic power, security, rent-seeking, status, and the like.

And yet if we carry on down this corrective road in a dogmatic, single-minded way, the result is hardly a well-rounded understanding. It is a self-destructive nihilism in thinking about institutions. If the normative purposes of institutions are regarded as pure facade, nothing more than masks to be continually stripped away so as to reveal interest group politics, legitimizing myths, self-interested bureaucratic survival strategies, and so on, there is really nothing much of substantive value to talk about. We will end up destroying the very basis for caring about institutions enough to want to think about them in the first place.

Let us turn again to the example of our public schools. As organizations, these schools give abundant evidence of being self-interested bureaucracies. It is also clearly the case that choices about their structure and operation are made through an interest-group politics involving administrators, teachers' unions, state legislators and governors, school boards, and other constituencies. The results are hardly rational, purpose-driven structures of action. On another reading, from a macrosociological view, it also seems fair to say that schools do serve as a ritual system of legitimation. On the input side, they garner broad public support by incorporating rationalized procedures independent of the practices' actually efficacy. On the output side they legitimate the whole rationalized modern social structure. Creating and validating categories of personnel and knowledge, schools allocate people to various status positions and sanction the approved forms of knowledge. These legitimating effects of schools construct a social reality that everyone—whether in or out of school—inhabits and accepts as true.[19]

All of these observations may be entirely accurate, but they do not get to the heart of what most people care about. They do not care primarily about schools as organizations. They care about schooling, the educational work that is supposed to be done in these organizations. That normative dimension of purpose is what is lost if we simply equate institutions with organizations, much less bureaucracies. It is precisely the requirements and exigencies of organizational life that people often find to be getting in the way of institutional values. No one seeks support for schools by claiming that bureaucratic self-interests will be served, that political constituencies will have their needs met, or that legitimating social myths will be reinforced. All that may be true, but it cannot be declared. It has to be disguised, and the cover-up is revealing. It does not mean that the institutional values are an empty facade. It means they are so real that they can be used to hide behind. La Rochefoucauld said that hypocrisy is the homage that vice pays to virtue. In this case, what the hypocrisy reveals is the widespread belief that a larger institutional purpose should infuse our schools' operation as organizations.

We noted earlier that any institution is likely to be a complex mixture of design and adaptation, of the formal and the informal. Likewise, an organization can be toward the more purely organizational end of a range. In that case it may be "valued" instrumentally, but this is a thinned-out form of valuing. Such an organization's worth consists in whether or not it helps you get what you want. At the other end of the range, an organization-as-institution will be valued intrinsically, not for its own sake, but for something more. It is participating in and expressing the stronger form of valuation that speaks to me about whether what I want is what I should want. We are now in the realm of substantive rather than merely instrumental rationality.

At this point, thinking about institutions takes on a growing and unfashionable moral quality. We begin pushing up against the limits of any academic perspective that views institutions as either organizations or as the rules of the game in which organizations are the players. The morality of contractual obligations, social roles, duty, and the like can be contained by rules. The morality of aspiration cannot.[20] Indeed, punctilious fulfillment of the letter of the law can easily destroy the spirit of the enterprise. Many of us have been in games in which some participant, a "stickler" for the rules and hypersensitive to any infraction, has ruined the game—the whole point of which was to have some competitive fun and not simply to obey the rules.

We are left searching for language to capture what is at stake here. What is this strong valuing that goes beyond instrumentalism? We might think of it as the claim beyond rule following that is made on us by a "practice." We might call it "the central logic," the "moral economy" or "animating idea" that justifies our loyalty to an institution.[21] Or we might get back to basics and simply call it the point of the thing. Whatever we might call it, it is what evokes our respect in depth.

Here we have reached a crucial inflection point in our consideration of institutions. In trying to combine the insights of the different schools of thought about institutions, we have now begun moving into territory beyond all the conventional school boundaries. To see why this is happening, it will help to revisit the best intellectually endowed school on the scene, the rational choice school.

Rational Calculation: Some Cases Worth Pondering

Whatever else you might think about the definitions and schools for thinking about institutions, it is fair to say that in the past generation none have dealt with the concept of institution in a more intellectually productive way than those in the "rational choice" school. Their combination of rigorous theoretical and empirical analysis is the kind of work that can win a person a Nobel Prize. It did just that for Douglass North and his research in economic history that applied rational choice theory and quantitative methods to explain economic and institutional change.

While the details can become quite complicated, we have already seen that this school's approach to institutions is rather straightforward and elegant. Here we need say only a little more to describe it. In a world of rational individuals interacting to pursue their self-interests, it is possible for everyone to gain by trading with each other. Left free from outside interference, the forces of competition will produce feedback that rewards the correct models of efficient behavior and punishes the faulty ways of pursing one's self-interest. This yields efficient markets and maximizes the aggregate income available in the gains from trade. However, this "neoclassical" result will occur only if bargaining is costless to the actors, and it almost never is. Significant "transaction costs" arise, for example, in gaining reliable information on what is being exchanged and in enforcing subsequent agreements. That is where institutions matter. They can be designed to establish rules that will help all parties acquire needed information, follow common procedures, define and protect property rights, enforce promise-keeping, and the like.

Without intending to denigrate the rich insights of this school, I think it is fair to say that by its own account, this approach eventually encounters a major barrier. In the hands of expert practitioners, the whole system for thinking about institutions as rules chosen by rational actors in pursuit of their interests unfolds with wonderful intellectual sophistication. But while the analytic framework drives forward with great rigor and insight, it ends up at a threshold before which it stands rather mute. At this point the way the rational human agent thinks about his interests has everything to say about what will happen, and the theory has little to say except that the agent will pursue his interests.

With apologies to Nobel Laureates in the field of rational choice economics, let me briefly use their own accounts to illustrate this threshold problem. We can first consider two specific cases that have been widely cited and then a more general statement of the problem.

Medieval "Street Cred"

The revival of European trade in the early Middle Ages strained the old reputation system that was built on continuing and direct interpersonal relationships (that is, I know these people and they are trustworthy trading partners). Now exchanges were occurring in much larger merchant communities and spreading across far longer distances. The simple system of reputations was no longer an adequate bond for supporting honest exchange among people whose reputations you did not know and whom you could not count on meeting again.

European merchants' response to this problem was to evolve a private code of commercial laws (*Lex Mercatoria*) using a local official, or "Law Merchant," to render judgments between disputing parties.[22] Significantly, the Law Merchant system had no way to enforce judgments against merchants, especially those from distant places. But it did provide a central place that provided reliable information on whether there were any outstanding judgments against a would-be trading partner. In this way, the institution of Law Merchants did provide sufficient, low-cost information to the members of the trading community that enabled them to know reasonably well the names of cheaters who should be boycotted. The infrequency of any given bilateral trading relationship did not matter once there was an efficient way that all the members of the trading community could be kept informed about each other's past behavior. Thus, rather than supplanting the reputation system, the Law Merchant institution made it more workable.

But this new institution in turn was workable only if the Law Merchant himself was not a cheat. So what keeps the rational Law Merchant fair and honest? After all, there is no meta–Law Merchant system for keeping people well informed about which Law Merchants should be boycotted. Of course, an instrumentally rational Law Merchant will want to guard his reputation in order to keep his business thriving. But if he extorts money by threatening a merchant's reputation, there is no easy way for the injured party to make this known to the large and far-flung community of traders; at best, extortion will have to be thwarted by rational victims realizing that payment will lead only to more extortion. The situation is even worse in the matter of bribery. It will be in the interest of any merchant with unpaid judgments to conceal that fact from trading partners. He will be ahead if he pays a portion of the judgment as a cover-up bribe to the Law Merchant. And why should not a rational Law Merchant take the bribe, since neither he nor the briber has an incentive ever to disclose the payoff?

At this point we can sense being pulled to step outside rational choice theory, and we may begin muttering things about how the judge needs to be somehow thinking about the duties of his position and the integrity of the Law Merchant system itself. As we shall see, our instincts are right.

Being Too Powerful for Your Own Good

A second widely cited case takes us to the emergence of something beginning to look like democracy in seventeenth-century England.[23] On the telling of rational choice theory, the story goes as follows. It is a time of civil war and massive upheavals at home, of more than a generation of religious-political wars on the Continent, and of British kings desperately needing more money. The moneyed interests represented in Parliament will gain from lending the money, but only if they can be sure their rights will be protected and the loans repaid.

The rub was that England's four Stuart kings of that century believed they were kings. They might need money, but they were still the sovereign power, and sovereignty could never be divided and shared. The difficulty is that with that kind of sweeping power you can allow yourself to renege on any loans, and so potential creditors have little reason to believe your promises to repay. Hence financial arrangements that could have been advantageous to both kings and financial backers in Parliament were not realized. The institutional solution was to design a new governmental system that would constrain the claims of royal sovereignty by transferring important powers to Parliament, thus making kingly promises to repay and protect property rights credible, and mutually beneficial deals with Parliamentary interests possible.

In the abstract, the king's power problem is a happy story of rational accommodation. What the rational choice model leaves unsaid is that the Stuart kings did not think of their interests in that enlightened way. Because they thought like kings, and not merchant traders, they acted like kings, and the "gains from trade" that the theory tells us were there, ripe for plucking, were a nonissue. And because of that, it took a royal beheading and several revolutions eventually to produce the institutional solution that schoolchildren read about (or at least used to read about) as the Glorious Revolution of 1688. The Stuart kings surely did calculate and reason. But they did so according to criteria that lay outside ordinary economic rationality.

So again we can sense being pulled outside rational choice theory to consider, for example, what was going on in their heads that this breed of Stuarts seemed unable to see beyond the end of their noses—indeed, to be unaware that their vision of absolute kingship had never prevailed in the development of English political institutions. It is a good question, but the mighty apparatus of rational choice theory stands mute at its asking.

Rulers Powerful Enough to Create Good Rules Don't Need To

We now come to the more general conundrum that arises at the intersection of rationality, power, and human agency. It has been said that "power is the ability to afford not to learn."[24] And yet a kind of learning is exactly what a rational choice view of institutions ultimately requires of rulers. Here is why.

As we have seen, rational choice theory teaches us that even with rigorous market competition among rational individuals, bargaining will entail significant transaction costs. Institutions are needed to establish rules that will help all the rational actors pursue their self-interests. The right institutions will provide these actors with what they need to act efficiently and thus produce the aggregate-level benefits that come from their individual microlevel calculations. Such institutions will provide access to reliable information for transactions, a common definition and protection of property rights, an unbiased enforcement of contracts and other legal promises, and so on.

The reality is that for such institutions to exist and successfully function, the coercive power of the state is required. If truth in advertising or protection of property rights is a take-it-or-leave-it voluntary affair, then there can be no real expectation of truth in advertising and no real property rights. More broadly, given the problem of collective action, powerful leaders can require contributions from participants to achieve public goods that will not otherwise be attainable because of everyone's incentive to be free riders in any voluntary system.

But if the rulers acquire enough power to enforce a good framework of rules, then they also have sufficient power to enforce rules serving only their own predatory interests. As Douglass North has said, "Institutions are not necessarily or even usually created to be socially efficient; rather they, or at least the formal rules, are created to serve the interests of those with the bargaining power to create new rules."[25] So here we truly do run up against it. Why should rulers powerful enough to underwrite institutions for the common good not use that power for their own immediate personal good, even if it is at the expense of the rest of society? When the rational choice theorist enters the throne room of the king, what answer can he give and justify from within the confines of his own theory?

As I said, my intention is not to belittle the important insights that rational choice theorists have contributed to the definition and analysis of institutions. However, by its own account, we do keep bumping up against a barrier where both the theory and its empirical analysis can go no further. What I am saying is that this barrier should really be seen as a threshold to step across, an entryway inviting us not only to think about institutions but also to consider, and value, what it is to think in an institutionally minded way. Step through the entryway I am proposing and we will see something more than individuals calculating how to maximize some interest. We will find humans beings, socially embedded, aspiring to live out some larger moral purposes. To be sure, that may sound hopelessly abstract. So let me end by offering an example addressing the issues left unanswered in the two preceding case studies, and then a similar counterpoint to the more general problem presented by the power to rule for good or ill.

The Law Merchant case left us asking why any rational holder of such a position should not extort funds or, easier still, accept bribes. The case of the king's power problem left us wondering why rulers should be so oblivious to their long-term interests. In the abstract there can be no end to such wondering. In the practice of ordinary life, even as expressed by extraordinary historic figures, a very great deal depends on how people choose to evaluate their obligations in light of some larger scheme of things. The external contextual pressures may be intense, but that inner voice, socially conditioned but not deterministically settled, still can have the last word.

George Washington's Mind

The questions left hanging in the Law Merchant and king's power cases can be illuminated by a somewhat related situation at the beginning of U.S. nationhood. In June 1775, a provincial colonel from Virginia, a man widely respected but with little reputation for military success, was appointed by Congress to be continental commander in chief of the emerging nation's ragtag army. As George Washington's greatest biographer put it:

> He had not gained this esteem by genius. ... Washington had won this place by the balance of his parts. In nothing transcendent, he

was credited with possessing in ample measure every quality of character that the administration of the army demanded. Already he had become a moral rallying post, the embodiment of the purpose, the patience and the determination necessary for the triumph of the revolutionary cause. He had retained the support of Congress and won that of New England in like manner and measure, by directness, by deference, and by manifest dedication to duty.[26]

Being given the position was one thing, but it was Washington who made the choices about what to do with it amid the operational realities of the times. What should a "rational" Washington do (other than not take the job in the first place)?[27]

In the critical years between the summers of 1775 and 1778, the new commanding general made not only military decisions but also political and institutional choices of immense long-run significance. The operational context was roughly as follows. Throughout this period the Congress and state governments consistently failed to provide the necessary support that Washington had been promised, to the point that he came to distrust all their promises. Experiencing almost war-ending shortages of men and supplies, Washington was repeatedly forced to retreat, delay, and maneuver, which aroused a steady drumbeat of political criticism for his failing to prosecute the war aggressively. Washington's confidences were repeatedly betrayed by leading politicians of the day. Pervasive legislative intrigues and military patronage cabals sought to undermine or to exploit his authority. His requests for guidance from Congress were often not responded to or were answered with useless prevarications. State commissions of politicians selected their local political favorites as the regimental officers of America's army. Election and promotion of Washington's general officers were in the hands of Congress, and he was expected to make the best of whatever such "leadership" was assigned to him. A number of these senior officers foisted on Washington owed their loyalties to political factions working behind his back, leading his own best major generals to protest or resign.

The ongoing fraudulent administration of army supplies was matched by parochial resentments and infighting among officers and enlistees from the different states. At the end of this period, in the winter of 1778, Washington watched his army all but starved and frozen to death as a result of what was—putting the very best face on it—gross incompetence in the civilian government's commissioning of supplies. Contrary to his expectations, America's army did not mutiny or disperse in that winter of sorrows.

As a context for rational choice there was another side to this picture. While Washington was desperate for resources to fight the war, as a practical matter he was also something approaching a sovereign power in the revolutionary regime. While Congress dithered and fled from place to place amid rumors of British attack, the only concrete force for the revolutionary cause was the army, and the only meaningful control of the army rested in Washington's hands. Insofar as the army held together, it did so primarily out of loyalty to and faith in him personally. Viewing this as a strategic context for rational choice, Washington was in an exceptionally favorable position. At a strictly venal level reminiscent of the Law Merchant problem, Washington was in a good situation to extort or be bribed through various side deals with the many contending parties. More than that, he was well positioned to enhance his power by using strategic moves to play off against each other contending political ambitions in the Congress and states. And well beyond that, Washington was in an excellent position to use his power as supreme military commander to present himself as a king-in-waiting; at that point in history there was no known alternative for thinking about executive power. And indeed, in the course of time a number of Washington's lieutenants saw it that way, urging a military coup to provide the manpower, supplies, and, above all, national resolve that were necessary to save the cause of the American Revolution.

Instead of making any of those moves, Washington consistently chose, so far as possible without losing the war, to remain dependent on a feckless and unreliable Congress. Remaining extremely careful in exercising powers his title seemed to confer, he did his best to consult Congress before acting. He refused to forage for supplies in the countryside without congressional authorization. He refused to take action against politically connected senior officers criticizing him behind his back, lest their needed services be lost to the army. He refused to answer political critics by making the obvious, true, and undoubtedly popular countercharge that failure to prosecute the war was due, not to a lack of generalship, but to the political incompetence and corruption in Congress as well as the unpatriotic selfishness of state politicians. He repeatedly asked Congress to clarify the scope of his authority in conducting the war. He refused to enter into political cabals and quietly exposed them when he could. He never threatened resignation to further his position (though as a younger man, intense regard for his honor and personal reputation would almost surely have led him to do so). Until Congress formally inquired of him, he deferred in recommending which of his generals should command major departments in the war. He accepted the worst of officers foisted on him by political patrons, offering them a cold, ceremonious civility.

Thus, even in the midst of the most extreme crisis, Washington continued to make a point of deferring to the civilian authority of the elected Congress. By the end of 1776 he was commander of a shadow army. Deserters (who absconded with their government-supplied arms and thus doubly weakened the army), regular soldiers refusing to reenlist, and state militias that would not leave home had created a condition such that the army and the Revolutionary cause faced certain defeat should the British attack. At this perilous moment, Washington took the initiative to recruit and bring into the army competent officers and the regimental troops who would follow them. And as the only possible way of holding the existing army together, Washington for the first time broke his rule and did not seek congressional authorization before offering bonuses ($6) to soldiers

would stay in the army for six weeks into the New Year.
.t Washington then immediately asked Congress to inform
.im if they disapproved of his initiative.

Unknown to Washington, Congress had days before finally
approved giving him general power to raise, equip, and manage
the army (limited to an emergency period of six months). The
covering letter from Congress said, "Happy it is for this country that the General of their forces can safely be entrusted with
the most unlimited power, and neither personal security, liberty,
nor property be in the least endangered thereby." Washington
responded: "Instead of thinking myself freed from all *civil* obligations by this mark of confidence, I shall constantly bear in
mind that as the sword was the last resort for the preservation
of our liberties, so it ought to be the first to be laid aside when
those liberties are firmly established."[28] And of course, four
years later, laying aside the sword and all claims to power is
exactly what Washington did, to the astonishment of Europe's
leaders.

In effect, Washington circumvented the "king's power
problem" cited above. He showed that he could be trusted
with power by not demanding it. Of course, it could be said
that in deferring to Congress Washington was behaving in a
strategically "rational" way. By eschewing claims to independent power he enhanced his chances of being entrusted with
more power. But to leave it there would be to remain willfully
oblivious to the central fact of the situation. Washington was
not being deferential to Congress. He was being deferential to,
and seeking to serve, the idea that Congress represented—
namely, republican self-government. One comes to the point
where the issue goes beyond thinking ratio-nally. The issue is
what it is that is worth thinking rationally about. Through it
all, Washington was intensely watchful, some would say obses-
sively careful, concerning the implications of every action on
his reputation—not his reputation for greatness or popular
approval but his reputation for being trustworthy in the service of duty. And that duty was to the cause of republican lib-

erty. Washington's behavior reflected the choices he thought that cause required of him.

Is my little portrait of Washington in action too good to be true? I do not think so. As we shall see in the next chapter, George Washington was drawing strength from a current of thought that had gripped the minds and hearts of many people in that generation of Americans-in-the-making. Along with others, Washington was thinking institutionally before there were formal political institutions to be thinking about. That is what made them all—from the highest to lowest social rank—"founders."

But I am also insisting in this book that we never lose sight of the individual and his or her responsibilities in relation to institutions. Washington was the indispensable man, the one person in a decisive position to turn the idea of republican self-government into reality. We can never know what other men who could well have been in his place—an Artemas Ward, Charles Lee, Israel Putnam, or Horatio Gates—might have done. But from his words and actions we can form a view of what Washington believed.

Washington believed that he had taken delivery of and been entrusted with something, that this something was a larger cause of immense intrinsic worth, and that his duty was to uphold this cause for its own sake, over the long term, and in such a way as to keep it alive without subverting its values. This was not just a morality of duty speaking but also a morality of aspiration, not a following of rules but a striving toward purpose. In the young nation there were no organized political institutions to speak of, but Washington was thinking institutionally. And because he was thinking that way, he chose to act as he acted.

★ ★ ★

We have spent most of this chapter concerned with how social scientists think about institutions. In one way or another, the various schools probably do manage to touch on how most of us in some casual manner think about these things. But thinking about institutions is not the same thing as thinking institutionally. To realize that fact we need not imagine ourselves to be

George Washington (although it is instructive to reflect on what one might have done in his shoes). We need only look at modern academia.

Clearly, if this chapter does nothing else, it shows that professors in the social sciences have expended considerable effort over the years in thinking about institutions. However, it is also painfully clear that very often professors (myself included) can be seen minimizing if not shirking their duties to their students and universities, duties that supposedly lie at the heart of any professor's calling to be part of an "institution" of higher learning. The professors' minds think about the thing—surely a worthwhile endeavor—but often they do not possess an internal point of view valuing the thing itself. Their minds are on institutions, but they are not institutionally minded.

Of course, my criticism presupposes that there really are purposes and standards that justify calling something an *institution* of higher learning, whether or not we petty careerist professors live up to those standards. It also presupposes that—to use the language of the schools—we are "agents" capable of living out a morality of aspiration. To be an agent is sometimes taken to mean simply one who acts on behalf of another person (hence the "agent/principal" problem in rational choice theory). But more fundamentally, to be an agent means to act purposively on behalf of a goal, policy, or principle. The schools tell us that institutions constrain and enable behavior, that socially constructed scripts are ever present in social action. All true. But people as agents do make their own choices in this institutional world tensioned between constraint and enablement. And the socially constructed scripts presented to us are hardly unambiguous guides to correct behavior.

To be an agent is to realize that, although embedded in the necessities of social circumstance, nature, and time, you are more than that. It is to know that you are a creature with the capacity to transcend those necessities and make history, the history that is the story of your personal life and, together with other human agents, the history that is the story of what humanity is making of itself. Deeper than the agent/principal issue is the agent/principle perspective. It presupposes that as beings (which by existing we surely are) we humans are moral agents. That is to say, by virtue of being human, we experience our existence as partaking in questions of right and wrong. To say human life is to say morally-implicated life. We often disagree on how to fill in those categories of right and wrong with actual behavior. But even the cruelest of our kind (take your choice: Hitler, Stalin, Mao, Pol Pot, Milosevic, Osama Ben Laden, Idi Amin, or any similar monster of recent fame) invariably resorts to moral categories for justification. In a twisted way, their incessant efforts to justify their cruelty by appealing to moral principles (remedying injustices, restoring purity, instituting a new world order, establishing God's law, and so forth) highlight the inescapable human participation in moral agency.

To gain a more rounded view of the subject, and one of greater relevance for our lives, we have to move beyond thinking about institutions and consider what it is to think as moral agents within a framework of institutional values. When Washington or anyone else is thinking institutionally, how are they thinking? What is this larger scheme of things involving agency and purpose? Exploring this internal point of view regarding institutions is the task of the next chapter.

Chapter Four
Being Institutionally Minded

In this chapter we consider a particular way of thinking. It is not so comprehensive as to deserve designation as a "worldview." And it is not systematic enough to be called a philosophy. It is tempting to call this way of thinking an "ethos." Anthropologists use that term to designate the evaluative character—the moral and aesthetic tone—of a given culture. However, that seems overly grand. As Clifford Geertz has said, a people's ethos is their underlying attitude toward themselves and their world that life reflects.[1] To be sure, the way of thinking I wish to talk about is evaluative in character, but it is more like a particular sensitivity than a comprehensive way of life. It is a sensitivity that coexists, competes with, and is often overwhelmed by other sensitivities carried around in our heads.

Probably the best we can do in modern English is to call this way of thinking a "stance" or "appreciative viewpoint."[2] As used here, appreciation does not mean simply an attitude of gratitude or admiration. An appreciative viewpoint is a way of being aware, a particular kind of sensitivity in forming judgments. The particular sensitivity to be discussed has to do with an appreciation that is institutional in its commitments. Venturing beyond the English language, the old medieval term *habitus* would serve well. It means a bent in one's disposition, something more socially conditioned than a personal preference but not so tightly structured as to render the individual a mere carrier of predetermined social norms.

As we noted at the outset of this book, the difficulty is that in these times we are trying to talk about a way of thinking that is sensed mainly as an absence. Institutional thinking seems to be one of the main things missing when all sorts of events repeatedly befoul American public life, involving both individuals and organizations. Its absence is a much felt presence, but we do not seem to have a way of discussing it. In this chapter I will try to describe the internal monologue that comes with being inside an institutional frame of mind and looking out. To visit this mental interiority is not a romantic adventure that is likely to produce box office hits or popular best-sellers. It is more like revisiting the rooms of a comfortable and forgotten old home. Institutional thinking is undramatic, unassuming, and unfashionable. That helps explain why we see so little of it.

The Internal Point of View

The last chapter ended by leaving an idea hanging: thinking about institutions is not the same thing as thinking institutionally. The latter involves shifting one's perspective to understand institutions from the inside out. This perspective is immensely important, and, to the great loss of all concerned, it is rarely discussed in our schools. That includes schools from the elementary level through college. Not being discussed, the whole subject of institutions shrivels toward an insignificance that is wholly at odds with human realities.

The conventional approach of the social sciences fails us at this point. To understand human affairs as they truly are, it is not enough to be a detached observer looking in. This gaze from the outside should not be disparaged, but it can never be sufficient to grasp the subject we are dealing with in this book. Moral agents thinking and acting within a framework of institutional values do not disclose their full character to the detached out-side gaze. There is a gap to be crossed between the life of moral commitment entailed in thinking institutionally and the life of detachment characterizing the academic social scientist. Deny-ing any inclination to pass judgment on the facts, the external observer parts company with the reality of people's lives. He fails to see that the object of his study differs in kind from that of the natural scientist.

What is missing is not simply a piece of academic curricu-lum. What is missing is something in the human curriculum that needs to be passed on to help young people get their bearings in the world. If our teaching considers institutions from only an outside, external viewpoint, we reinforce the prevailing tendency to dismiss the meaningfulness of institutional values. Understand-ing from the inside lets us see how people use such value com-mitments to appraise their own and others' behavior, to give rea-soned meaning to the decisions and actions that they take in life.[3] By omitting the internal point of view, we indirectly teach and reinforce the idea that our social existence is merely a succession of fluid, revocable associations of convenience and arbitrary per-sonal tastes.

While thinking "about" institutions is an intellectual project conducted by professional academics, thinking institutionally is something both broader and deeper. It is about a way of carry-ing on in the real world, and we all do it to a greater or lesser extent—at the office, in family relations, in the public square. Whatever academics might have to say about institutions, an institutional way of thinking concerns value-laden attachments that we all accept, refuse, or negotiate in one way or the other in our lives. That is why the issue of thinking institutionally is bound up in not only an academic curriculum but a human one: it carries great consequence for grounding our self-under-standing as moral agents. Thinking about institutions may make you a social scientist, but thinking institutionally can actually help make you a more fulfilled human being. That is a large and rather arrogant claim, and my hope is that by the time you come to the end of this book you will be in a good position to weigh its merits.

Let me put the point another way. To think about art is not the same thing as having an artistic view of the world, just as thinking about science is not identical to thinking like a scientist. To think about religion is clearly not the same thing as being religious in your approach to daily life. Likewise, as I have learned over the years, to think about marriage is certainly not the same thing as thinking like a married person. Indeed, the more you think in the abstract about marriage (prenuptial contracts, child custody issues, joint property arrangements, and so on) the less likely you may be able to embrace the full human commitment of being a married person.

The sorry fact is that "thinking about" may actually diminish capacities for "thinking in" institutional terms. The academic approach of the schools has the effect of rendering everything into a subject/object relationship. It tends to drain away the capacity truly to appreciate what it means to mentally inhabit a world endowed with institutional values. Thinking about institutions is not the same thing as thinking institutionally because "thinking about" does not tell us what it is like for a person to go around with presuppositions of the relevant institutional values and purposes in his or her head. Accepting and participating in those values and purposes as a moral agent is what makes you a part of the institution. And, reciprocally, it makes the institution an important part of who you are, even though it need never fully define you.

It might be objected that scientists, artists, and, yes, even married persons think in many different ways. And in a behavioral-descriptive sense, that is of course true. Inside institutions we can find people driven by considerations of personal self-interest, disinterested concern for others, conformity to peer pressure, unthinking habit, and much more. But to stop there leaves us on the descriptive periphery of the subject. It says nothing about the institutional point of view itself and simply misdirects our attention to incidental variations in personal behavior.

An internal perspective shows something different. It is a stance/appreciative viewpoint asserting that by virtue of participating in an institutional form of life, there are more and less appropriate ways of doing things. These obligations are a kind of internal morality that flows from the purposive point of the institution itself. An institution brings expected conduct within a normative order that has its own history, irrespective of the fact that the actual behavior of various human beings may not conform to those expectations. And I suspect that if, rather than trying to score intellectual points, we are seriously reflecting on our own life experiences, we all know that the "internal point of view" can be quite real. When the house is on fire, a person who rushes to save the family photo album rather than the television set or latest game player is expressing a form of institutional thinking. That person has thought with a familial appropriateness.

If all of this seems too vague, we might return to the "hard" sciences and consider the contrast between thinking *about* physics, chemistry, biology, and the like and thinking like a scientist engaged in investigating those matters. By invoking the term "thinking like a scientist" I do not mean that there is some unique scientific mind or psychological makeup possessed by people called scientists. It is true that some champions of science like to hold on high the model scientist who exhibits a psychological state of disinterested objectivity, rigorously discarding preconceptions and personal preferences as he or she proceeds down the path of neutral scientific inquiry. But that kind of psychologism is not how science works.[4]

It is closer to the mark to say that thinking like a scientist means accepting a method of inquiry, the scientific method. However, that too is often said quite glibly, providing a recipe for science fair projects but little idea of what acceptance of the method implies. What the method really means is that science is a social institution. As a practical matter, the social group composed over the generations of those agreeing with the purpose of the scientific enterprise and submitting to its rules in pursuit of that purpose constitutes the institution that is science.

The scientific method is a set of rules of procedure, a methodology. But the rules are not the institution. The rules are choices made by people engaged in the scientific enterprise. The community of people lays down requirements to act in certain ways in order to pursue the purpose that the people in this enterprise hold in common. That purpose, labeled the "advancement of science," is to search for universal laws and causal explanations regarding how the physical world truly works. Such knowledge is acquired by observations, hypothetical statements, predictions, and experiments interrogating the physical world. These supply the materials, not the method, for doing science and thinking like a scientist.

The scientific method stipulates the manner in which science permits one to learn from these materials. This method for acquiring reliable knowledge requires that all statements about how the physical world works must be capable of repeatable tests that could falsify the claims of any observation, experiment, hypothesis, or prediction. In other words, any claim of scientific knowledge must be made in a public—social—way that is capable of being examined by others committed to testing the claim against evidence from the same physical world. These others may want to do so out of personal spite, self-centered ambition, idealistic causes, or any number of other reasons. The issue is not one of motivation but the method of intersubjective testability. Any general statement that is not capable of being tested for refutation is not considered a valid scientific statement.

The possibility of falsification is central because no number of confirming observations can establish a generalization beyond doubt, and we all wish to confirm what we believe is true. So there is that ever-present human temptation to resort to confirming evidence and avoid anything to the contrary. But only one contradictory piece of evidence can be sufficient to disprove a generalization. The scientific method, for the sake of seeking truth, fully embraces that need to work against the easy grain of human gullibility and self-validation. In this sense, while the aim of science is to discover empirical truth, it can be approached only indirectly by eliminating what is false.

This means that moral obligation lies at the heart of science as a social institution. The scientific method depends on something more than the mere possibility of falsification. It requires human beings—the scientists who make up this community—who are positively committed to seeking contrary evidence and who reject any effort to protect scientific statements from falsification (for example, by changing definitions, bringing in ad hoc hypotheses, using authority to dismiss evidence, personally attacking critics, or suppressing inconvenient facts). The subsidiary rules of science can be debated and changed, but to reject this moral obligation to seek the truth through falsification is to abandon science itself and launch into a different game.

We know that in practice, scientists often do not work in the way I have just indicated. Scientific organizations and research programs (which are not the same thing as the institution of science) can be authoritarian, elitist, and closed-minded. Theories become established and "normal science" often proceeds in a rather uncritical way, as if the prevailing model had been verified by experience and needed no further scrutiny. However, the point is that in the scientific community as a whole, this intellectual lassitude and dogmatic acceptance remains continuously vulnerable to public challenge in light of new evidence. Within the self-corrective process of science itself, it remains possible for observations to accumulate and deepen doubt about the scope of the old model's applicability. The stage is then set for a revolutionary upheaval that can replace the old models with new ones. Such scientific revolutions can and do happen because the core purposes and obligations to truth in the scientific enterprise have remained intact.[5]

To a nonscientist, all this might seem rather austere, impersonal, and, well, "scientific." But please consider more carefully the "purposed" nature of this group of people who submit to the scientific method. Across the generations, theirs is a magnificent expression of the human spirit. To think scientifically is to launch on a quest that values, above all things, truth. It is to trust that the scientific search for truth will be granted success by powers beyond our command. In confident faith, beyond any possibility of evidence, such thinking presupposes that there is intelligible meaning in the natural world itself, an underlying order to things that is universal and eternal. This quest does not begin in rational calculation or critical analysis. It begins with human wonderment at the world and a prerational appreciation for the beauty of intellectual order.[6]

But there is something going on in science that is still more astonishing than that. To think scientifically is to trust wholeheartedly that the presumed order of the natural world is accessible to man's scientific investigation—that any truths about the nature of things expressed in empirical data can actually be grasped by the powers of the human mind. The social institution of science, with its framework of moral agency and purpose, shows that among the most incomprehensible things about the universe is the fact that there is a creature in it that should imagine it is comprehensible. Unknowingly, because they have never been taught this way, students in tens of thousands of annual science fair projects are being asked to participate in a community of moral agency and purpose that endorses certain emotions and values as correct. To think within the institutional framework of science is to endorse a wonder, passion, and faith that do in fact glorify the human spirit.

I hope that this example from the "hard" sciences will help to clarify the shift to an internal perspective that I am trying to present. Here, as in other areas, we are struggling with a certain deficiency in language. If the text you are reading were written in another language (say, Greek or German) we could use different verbs to distinguish the various meanings of the term "to know" with regard to institutions. There could be a verb for "know" as in an external observer seeing and noticing something. There could be another word for "know" in the sense of recognizing and comprehending the features of what you have seen in the first sense. Both of these stances of "knowing about" were the subject of the last chapter. However, there could also be a word "know" that means to understand something from the inside, to know by partaking in the known. That knowing-as-participating-in is what we are trying to deal with in this chapter. To think in an inside way means to "know something" as in fully experiencing it and not just thinking about it, to have an intimate engagement rather than an intellectual encounter with something. The internal point of view gives us access to what it means to think institutionally, or as expressed at the beginning of this book, to have "respect in depth."

These distinctions may make sense to you, but in trying to use them we immediately run into a problem. To be sure, thinking institutionally is not the same thing as thinking about this or that institution. However, institutional thinking usually occurs in the context of some particular institution, and without this particularity, there is only so much that reasonably can be said on the subject. But this still leaves some things that can be said, and my task here is to try to distill common features of institutional thinking. The institution in question may be an organized social structure (such as the court system, university, or church) or a social practice (such as a given profession, rules of legal procedure, or religious ritual). Here we are trying to work above these particularities and sketch some important general features of mental life inside things institutional.

Some Family Features

We will begin by way of negation and then move on to three more positive elements of thinking institutionally. The various features to be discussed are obviously overlapping, and they probably have to be in order to constitute what is a single appreciative viewpoint. It would be a mistake to try to turn these distinctions into sealed compartments.

What It Is Not

There are two major issues to observe concerning what institutional thinking is not. In the first place, thinking institutionally is not the same thing as thinking in organizational or bureaucratic terms. Our modern society has developed through immense organizations for production, consumption, communication, entertainment, warfare, and the like. This has tempted many people into equating bureaucratic power structures with institutions. That makes it easy for critics to see the notion of institutional loyalty as just another expression of the blighted life of William Whyte's "organization man," the soulless modern who has "left home, spiritually as well as physically, to take the vows of organization life."[7]

However, institutional thinking has to do with living committed to the ends for which organization occurs rather than to an organization as such. To the institutionalist inside it, the organization has a surplus of meaning insofar as it is seen to serve a valued cause in some important way. Bureaucratic organizations in particular are tools that need to be held to their right use in light of their larger purpose. Thus institutional loyalty is not necessarily the same thing as organizational loyalty, and in practice the two can be in profound conflict. For example, it is clear that J. Edgar Hoover became very adept at thinking organizationally to protect his bureaucratic empire, and in doing so did long-term damage to the institutional qualities of the FBI as a law-enforcement agency. By contrast, FBI agent Coleen Rowley brought forward to her superiors information on the agency's pre-9/11 failures because "the issues are fundamentally ones of integrity and go to the heart of the FBI's law enforcement mission and mandate."[8] It was a career-ending choice to put thinking institutionally morally ahead of thinking organizationally.

Institutions usually are associated with particular organizations that are at least formally charged with pursuing certain ends. In the next chapter we will have more to say about the distinction between "good" and "bad" institutions. Here we need to recognize that however good the institution and its organizational manifestation might be, there is no morally simple way of deciding the limits of loyalty. Group loyalty can too easily become the highest form of morality. Leaders can have a knack for exploiting the feeling that everyone ought to be a "team player." When does the whistleblower blow too quickly or too often? What line will tell us that a police force, military unit, or teachers' union has gone too far in protecting their own? Is nepotism an authentic form of family loyalty? Answers to such questions have to be sought by consulting the larger purposes of any institution for genuine human well-being.

To be sure, wondering about one's duty in a particular case is often nothing more than an attempt to explain it away. But there are also difficult situations where there is no obvious answer. Thinking institutionally means being mindful of one's duty. And that means accepting that there can be anguishing choices to be made in matters of personal duty and organizational loyalty. To deny the tragic quality of such situations will simply throw us into worse errors. Like Virgil's Aeneas, the dutiful institutionalist may well have to pass through the sad vale of soul-making.[9]

★ ★ ★

In the second place, thinking institutionally is not the same thing as "critical thinking," a term that has now come into much fashion in academia. In other words, the central impulse among institutionalists is not to rigorously question and challenge everything presented. There is no agenda of "critical" analysis to unmask, demystify, and expose with a "hermeneutics of suspicion."[10] On the contrary, institutional thinking offers some good reasons to be rather suspicious of unremitting suspicion. It considers any call to question everything and challenge all claims based on authority to be errant, self-destructive nonsense. We should consider more closely why this is so, although I realize that at this point I may be burning a good many bridges with any academic audience.

★ ★ ★

Since the 1980s the "critical thinking movement" has been an important influence on curriculum reform and teaching assessment throughout K–12 public schools, as well as in our colleges and universities. Of course, if critical thinking is taken to mean using one's mind in a clear, careful, inquiring, and logical way, then there cannot be much room for objection. It is really not saying much more than that a critical thinker is a good thinker. For several millennia teachers have been trying to help students acquire the skills and attitudes needed to move in that laudable direction. It is equivalent to teaching competence in reading or writing and obviously useful in any subject.[11]

However, educational malpractice begins to emerge when this commonsense view becomes a device for teaching that the only really intelligent thinker is the critical thinker. When critical thinking is equated with the one right way of being intelligent, we are left with a major problem. Most of the experts in the forefront of the critical thinking movement in our schools realize that there is no conception of moral agency or purpose necessarily associated with this skill.[12] The whole business of teaching critical thinking really has nothing to say about what one should do with this ability. It may just as easily make a person a better scoundrel as a better citizen. It is comparable to teaching the scientific method as a technique and remaining oblivious to the moral obligations and purposes of science as a social institution. Devoid of institutional appreciations, the vaunted intelligence associated with critical thinking is really a way of not knowing.

Consider the recipe that advocates of the critical thinking movement present as the essential steps in effective thinking and problem solving. Curriculum guides and teachers' workbooks relish acronyms, and in this case the widely marketed recipe is called IDEALS (an irony I could not have invented). The IDEALS model advocates the following six steps for critical thinking:

- **I**dentify the problem
- **D**efine the context
- **E**numerate choices
- **A**nalyze options
- **L**ist reasons, and
- **S**elf-correct

If you are thinking critically about critical thinking, you will notice that something important is missing. The schema identifies everything surrounding the moment of decision, but says nothing about making the decision itself. With the lists of choices, analyzed options, and reasons spread out in front of me, what should guide my decision? Is there an ethic requiring something of me? Is there a tradition of learning and wisdom outside myself to draw on? Is there some community to which I owe allegiance? Are there institutional values deserving my assent for the sake of sustaining some common way of life? From my IDEALS recipe I might reasonably infer that the answer to all such questions is no. There are no substantive criteria that should be consulted or followed in making the decision. There is only the disembodied act of choosing. By his own reasoning and observations of the world, the critical thinker possesses within himself all he needs for problem solving.

To this vacuousness the institutionalist wholeheartedly objects. If for no other reason, he objects because the inevitable implication of such teaching is to destroy the integrity—the tied-togetherness—of what it means to be human. The implication is that we should teach youth that to be intelligent—that is, to be a critical thinker—is something that happens in one compartment of your life. In another compartment, presumptively not based on intelligence, is the ethical dimension that might tell you what critical thinking should be used for. It follows that if moral agency is not a matter of intelligent judgment, it must be a residual compartment dominated by irrational emotion, arbitrary traditions, or personal tastes needing no intelligent justification. Perhaps the academic champions of critical thinking do not mean to do so, but they are teaching young people to think of themselves not as persons but as disassembled, hermetically sealed compartments of critical intelligence, personal moral preference, and basic instinct.

As a curriculum reform initiative, the "critical thinking movement" is a reflection of larger intellectual fashions in leading academic circles. There the "critical" perspective is invoked to make it the main goal of education to reveal the reality-creating social, historical, and psychological forces that shape our lives. These forces are unveiled and shown to be mechanisms for exercising power and gaining submission to the disguised will of cultural authorities. Generally speaking, the resulting cultural inheritances are shown to be narrow, oppressive, and patriarchal. Unless one is deconstructing them, reading the canonical text is a form of indoctrination. But above all, the critical insight is that all cultural inheritances are something to see through, go behind, and get over. Only after escaping the grip of authority can you create an authentic, independent life for yourself.

Thus the critical thinking movement presents itself as going to "the heart of education . . . where traditional advocates of a liberal education always said it was."[13] What the leading lights of modern liberal education set as their objective is essentially the opposite of thinking institutionally. For example, the Harvard faculty's most recent formulation of its hopes for the new general education curriculum and the broader Harvard College experience goes as follows:

> The aim of a liberal education is to unsettle presumptions, to defamiliarize the familiar, to reveal what is going on beneath and behind appearances, to disorient young people and to help them to find ways to reorient themselves. A liberal education aims to accomplish these things by questioning assumptions, by inducing self-reflection, by teaching students to think critically and analytically, by exposing them to the sense of alienation produced by encounters with radically different historical moments and cultural formations and with phenomena that exceed their, and even our own, capacity fully to understand.[14]

Amidst all this unsettling, defamiliarizing, disorienting, assumption-questioning, and induced alienation, we are left with a troublesome question. How and where are students going to get the promised help "to find ways to reorient themselves"? Where are the compass bearings for this reorientation to come from? It surely will not come from the "alienation" produced by encountering what we lack the capacity to understand. It would appear that the great task of liberal education is to leave students with no solid sense of reality. And then let them figure out things for themselves.

The truth, critically understood, is that "traditional advocates of liberal education" have clearly not "always" had this view. Their view has been more like what the Renaissance humanist Pier Paolo Vergerio pictured:

> We call those studies liberal, then, which are worthy of a free [*liber*] man: they are those through which virtue and wisdom are either practiced or sought, and by which the body or mind is disposed towards all the best things. From this source people customarily seek honor and glory, which for the wise man are the principle rewards of virtue. Just as profit and pleasure are laid down as ends for illiberal intellects, so virtue and glory are goals for the noble.[15]

Hence it is not surprising that institutional thinking is at odds with the critical thinking movement in whatever its modern guises. The movement's advocates say that at its core, critical thinking is "judgment that is purposeful and self-regulatory." But it is judgment that does not endorse, or even recognize, any purpose beyond itself. The "self-regulatory" quality of its judgments is better described as self-referential, for it presumes that no external correctives from the surrounding material of history, religion, or culture are necessary. It is an educational agenda that teaches students how to fit into a larger culture that is telling you to believe whatever you like, but trust nothing. At often very high tuition rates, our children are being taught to take their places in the upper ranks of a culture that essentially distrusts itself.

Young people on the receiving end of this treatment in our high schools and colleges are never encouraged to be critical about the critical thinking movement itself. Students are to trust in the authority of the self-proclaimed "experts" urging critical thinking on them. Let us return to a founding document of the critical thinking movement cited earlier, *Critical Thinking: A Statement of Expert Consensus for Purposes of Educational Assessment and Instruction*. Who are these experts? Should it worry us that only two are from the natural sciences? That none are from outside the United States? That there is no empirical evidence offered to support their claims about the benefits to students of teaching the proposed critical thinking curriculum? And yet, if you think critically about such critical thinking, you must ask, What is the warrant for these people teaching me that this critical view is the one right way of thinking?

Likewise, a Harvard freshman could legitimately wonder about what wellsprings of knowingness justify such a determined and well-paid effort by the professorate to unsettle, defamiliarize, and disorient young minds. Why should we accept the belief that all beliefs are personal and culturally subjective—all beliefs, that is, except this one that our academic seers are feeding us? In late 2007 our imaginary freshman was told by Harvard's new president that "truth is an aspiration, not a possession. Yet in this we—and all universities defined by the spirit of debate and free inquiry—challenge and even threaten those who would embrace unquestioned certainties. We must commit ourselves to the uncomfortable position of doubt, to the humility of always believing there is more to know, more to teach, more to understand."[16]

But wait, our young novice thinker might say. Why does the spirit of debate and free inquiry in a university mean we must commit ourselves to doubt as an unquestioned certainty? To be sure, truth is our right aspiration, but whence the dogma that it can never be our possession? And why assume that because we believe certain things are true we cannot also believe there is always more to know, teach, and understand?

Although a person's constantly questioning, skeptical awareness is taken by the critical thinking movement to be the very
hallmark of intelligence, the truth is that our leading modern
intellectuals, who are the sort of people who write about institutions, are a peculiar social type with a particular outlook that
is itself rarely critically examined. While they champion the idea
of self-consciously thinking about and questioning everything
we are doing, they do not live the game they are preaching.
They—just like the rest of us—spend their lives uncritically
doing most things from habit. We have in fact already surveyed
that ground in the earlier comments in Chapter 2 regarding the
burden and impracticality of such a hypercritical intellectual
agenda.

Since there is much about thinking institutionally that is not
focused on thinking critically about what you are doing, today's
"advanced" academic perspective subtly but consistently devalues
institutional commitments. It does so by dismissing or holding in
low esteem one of the central operations of such commitments—
namely, the internalization of norms of social usage to the point
of habitual practice. As one of Britain's more exceptional intellectuals put it almost a century ago: "It is a profoundly erroneous truism, repeated by all copybooks and by eminent people when they
are making speeches, that we should cultivate the habit of thinking of what we are doing. The precise opposite is the case. Civilization advances by extending the number of important operations which we can perform without thinking about them."[17]

However, if we leave it at this, institutional thinking risks
being misunderstood as simple conformity, either to what some
tradition tells you to do or to what everyone else is doing. The
truth is that it is precisely against such a loss of "will to meaning" that institutions stand guard. Modern prejudices to the contrary, thinking institutionally is still thinking. Rather than being
mindless, it means being mindful in certain ways, exercising a
particular form of attentiveness to meaning in the world. A certain kind of intelligence is required to appreciate such meaning.
The real choice is not between critical thinking and mindless,

_..tual behavior. It is deciding which habits are worthy to be embraced.

Institutional Thinking as Faithful Reception

As a basic orientation toward life, institutional thinking understands itself to be in a position primarily of receiving rather than of inventing or creating. The emphasis is not on thinking up things for yourself, but on thoughtfully taking delivery of and using what has been handed down to you. In taking delivery, institutionalists see themselves as debtors who owe something, not as creditors to whom something is owed. As debtors they have been freely given a world charged with meaning and calls to commitment. What is on offer is an invitation to engagement that goes well beyond self-engagement. Faithful reception gives life meaning by establishing a connection with exterior referents from the past that have, in a sense, already gone beyond and outlived you, and done so to your benefit. This view of indebtedness was expressed by a young Abraham Lincoln as he spoke about the political institutions he saw around him in 1838:

> We find ourselves under the government of a system of political institutions, conducing more essentially to the ends of civil and religious liberty, than any of which the history of former times tells us. We, when mounting the stage of existence, found ourselves the legal inheritors of these fundamental blessings. We toiled not in the acquirement or establishment of them—they are a legacy bequeathed to us by a once hardy, brave, and patriotic, but now lamented and departed race of ancestors.[18]

So it is that in receiving a benefit with gratitude and faithfulness, a person repays the first installment on his debt.

Because the known ways are valued, thinking institutionally gives no special premium to newness and originality for its own sake. There is no esteem to be gained by thinking up things for yourself. Instead, a person who is thinking institutionally has entered into a preexisting normative field meant to guide the choices of agents within the given institution, regardless of their private preferences. Not the only job, but the job most at hand in all respects and times is learning how to play the game well, with an excellence that goes beyond rote obedience to the rules of the game. A player respecting the game of basketball may not know who Dr. Naismith was or the original rules about peach baskets, or that the game once had nothing to do with slam dunks and jump shots. Innovation is not meant to change the game. Legitimate innovation is meant to realize, with greater skill and fidelity, the larger potential of what the game is. In a line from Goethe that the late Jaroslav Pelikan liked to quote, "What you have received as heritage, take now as task and thus you will make it your own."

Here too, modern minds can find this emphasis on receiving to be quite strange, to say the least. When some issue arises, we expect to consult different opinions, consider alternatives, and come up with a working solution, preferably something new and innovative. From the institutionalist perspective, things are different. What has been received from those who preceded us carries a presumed weightiness. It is precisely this weighty, rooted quality of what has been given to us that makes it rest heavily in the working of our minds. The inheritance does not present itself as something to be regarded as a passing intellectual fancy, mood swing, or convenient opportunity for personal development (although it surely is the latter). Having a realistic, sober view of our human condition, the institutionalist understands that people usually have a greater need to be reminded than to be liberated.

To repeat, this does not mean closing off thought to any form of innovation. Quite the contrary. In Giuseppe Di Lampedusa's novel *The Leopard,* the young nephew puts the point well to his complacent, aristocratic uncle (I paraphrase): "If we want things to stay the same, there are going to have to be some changes." Precisely because it regards itself as a legatee of something of great value, institutional thinking eagerly seeks to understand what has been received in light of new circumstances that are always intruding. Without appropriate adaptations, the legacy cannot be preserved.

To be willing to submit to what has been received is a distinctly unfashionable idea in contemporary society. That is why the canon of Western literary classics has aroused such controversy in modern academia. It is why in all the arts, modern critics have had a field day cutting the masters down to size and declaring "genius" to be merely a socially constructed category.[19] Scratch below the surface and you will see that the difficulty is not really that the allegedly "great" works were created by European white males. If Shakespeare were someday discovered to be a black woman, the problem with honoring the excellence of the classics would still be the same. It would be the problem of submitting to the authority of Shakespeare and his, or her, brilliance.

The institutionalist values and is willing to submit to authority, and to admire the excellences of what has been delivered to him. However, submitting and admiring does not mean being servile and retrograde. It does mean having quite modest expectations of what is to be gained by historically careless innovation or by valuing newness for its own sake. More than that, because the internal perspective of thinking institutionally regards some things as givens that have been handed down to us (such as the essential mission of a business, an artistic style, the meaning embedded in a tradition, ritual, or, in a politician like Lincoln's case, the idea of the Union), there is something against which to be adaptable. Indeed, an otherwise unavailable space for adaptability and even playfulness is opened up precisely because one is working within a known context of rules and values. Whether playing at sports, music, mathematics, creative writing, architecture, or any other creative activity of the human spirit, improvisation is intelligible and possible because there is an inherited background against which to improvise and be playful.

The contrast between thinking institutionally and thinking in line with current intellectual fashions is stark. The postmodern stance of anti-institutional thinking rejects all such inherited values as cultural oppressions. Meaning is to be found only in self-creation, not faithful reception of something beyond oneself. As a result, the anti–institutionalist outlook has no capacity for either playful improvisation or genuine admiration. Instead, it has only the drab promise of disoriented, anarchic, and ultimately meaningless self-expression. Perhaps that is why so many of the sophisticated thinkers embracing the postmodern movement exhibit, not a sense of joyful exhilaration at their liberation, but a deep, unrequited sadness.[20] And even if the professors put a brave face on the idea of living without roots, the sadness is likely to creep into their students.

Institutional Thinking as Infusions of Value

It has been famously observed that to institutionalize is to "infuse with value beyond the technical requirements of the task at hand."[21] This is a helpful view because it points toward the distinction between strictly instrumental attachments needed to get a particular job done and the deeper commitments that express one's enduring loyalty to the purpose or purposes that lie behind doing the job in the first place. Such a commitment may entail ongoing loyalty to some organized group or process, but the sense of attachment that marks institutional thinking requires us to go a good deal farther down this path.

The shape of that longer journey becomes clear if we ask where the infusion of value is coming from. If it is simply a matter of the individual actor's injection of meaning, then we are implicitly relegating institutions to objects of psychological purchase that people choose to make based on some sort of pleasure/pain calculation. For example, the devout sports fan may in this sense infuse the game with value, his payoff being to "get a kick out of it." Yet, it is clear that such a fan may also have little interest in—and may easily behave in ways harmful to—this given sport as an institution. His self-centered enthusiasm as a fan is such that he behaves like a lout in the stands, potentially discrediting the game in the eyes of all who see him. Likewise, the most talented player of a game may achieve glorious records and still be an utter failure as an upholder of the game as an institution. I think that is what Ryne Sandberg meant in the passage quoted at the outset of this book. As he saw it, the honor of being elected to the Baseball Hall of Fame was not a reward. It was a validation for doing what you are supposed to do out of respect for the game.

In other words, institutional thinking is about value diffusion as well as infusion. Institutions diffuse values by connecting a person to something that goes beyond the self-life. They make claims on one's thinking to acknowledge, and then through choices and conduct, to help realize some normative order reflected in the task of upholding the institution and what it stands for. Institutions embody principles that guide and are necessary for institutional existence. It is not enough that an institutional purpose speaks to you. It must speak into you. It is the work of moral agency to try to live out what that larger purpose is saying.

Institutions embody what the philosopher Charles Taylor has termed "strong evaluations." As he puts it, these "involve discriminations of right or wrong, better or worse, higher or lower, which are not rendered valid by our own desires, inclinations or choices, but rather stand independent of these and offer standards by which *they* can be judged" (my emphasis).[22] These intrinsic values imply relations of obligation, not calculations of convenience or personal preference. They demand that primary attention be given to what is appropriate rather than to what is personally expedient. From inside an institutional worldview, one is moved by a central fact—that there is something estimable and decisive beyond me and my immediate personal inclinations. In approaching a major choice, the question is not, How can I get what I want? It is the duty-laden question that asks, What expectations and conduct are appropriate to my position and the choices I might make? What is it, larger than myself, into which I am drawn? And attracted by the light of its value, what *should* I want? The particulars will vary with the institution, but generally speaking, all institutions offer answers to such questions, questions that modern societies have often forgotten how to ask.

If merely thinking "about" institutions, we would now have reached the doorway into a very complicated discussion. Behind this door lie distinctions between values and norms, the moral and the ethical. Here, in analyzing the normative status of institutions, we would find ourselves weighing arguments about the primacy of the right or the good. Are individuals lashed from behind by norms, duties, the right? Or are they pulled from ahead by the attraction of values, aspirations, the good? In an age of skeptical self-awareness, how shall we justify choosing how to choose? On what basis should we prefer the claims of Kantian deontology or the claims of pragmatic consequentialism? Difficult questions to be sure, and if one is working from the framework of the critical thinking or cultural deconstruction movements, it seems that there are no rational, intersubjectively verifiable standards for choosing how to choose. This is why the only conclusion postmodern thinkers can seem to come to is the advice that, through acts of will, a person should create his or her life as a work of art.

To our great good fortune, given the internal point of view we are pursuing here, there is no need to tie ourselves up in such intellectual knots. These intricacies of justification, however intellectually interesting they might be in their unending mental scrollwork, are more of a distraction than an aid to understanding.[23] In the action-based life world that gives rise to institutional thinking, we are not working off premises of skepticism and introverted self-awareness. We are institutionally minded and looking outward to the world. And from this perspective it is easy to appreciate the continuous interplay between, on the one hand, the attractions and aspirations by which institutional purposes draw us and, on the other, the norms and duties that consequentially make themselves felt in our daily lives. Obeying the rules of grammar and respecting forms of syntax are one thing. Pursuing the vaguer and more morally charged goal of good writing or even literary excellence is another. However, these are not two opposing things, just different and related things. Properly appreciated, the two activities are complementary and capable of enriching each other.

The law as an institution is a good example of such complementary interplay. Seen up close in its daily operations, the legal system occupies itself in what appear as procedural routines virtually devoid of moral content. Day in and day out the attempt goes on to govern human behavior by the application of coercive rules. Even here, however, a certain "inner morality" is demanded for the law to actually be law. This morality is thin, to be sure, but it is what is required by the concept of law, especially if that concept includes the idea that law is something meant to be obeyed. Thus, if there is to be law—an application of coercive rules to govern people's behavior—among the requirements are that the rules are (1) publicly known, (2) not contradictory or retroactive, (3) capable of being obeyed as a practical matter, (4) stable enough to guide action, and (5) administered in a consistent way with what the rules say.[24] Those are internal "ought" requirements implied by even the most amoral understanding of what law "is."

However, to stop there would be like confining our understanding of writing to the rules of grammar, or of science as an institution to the routines of the scientific method. Looking from the outside we can see a conceptual separation of law and morals. The law is not a device to enforce anyone's moral blueprint for life. However, from the internal point of view, the law as an institution means that one is participating in something that was brought into being and continues to exist precisely for moral purposes. It is not a matter of law imposing morality; law *is* the expression of a moral viewpoint. It expresses an aspiration for justice applying to all persons through the rule of law. In ordering human affairs, this is what the institution of law is seeking to "see to."[25] It is at the heart of why human beings struggled to create, and continue struggling to uphold, a *legal* order as distinct from a discretionary order (law is whatever the ruler decides) or a customary order (law is whatever rules have always existed). Legal rules—not arbitrary princely whims or vague ancestral traditions—are to function as the governing reasons for decisions and action. The institution of law is infused with and diffuses value because of this faith that the rule of law will do best at pursuing the moral goal of equal justice.

If the law seems too abstract, we might return to a more emotionally risky example: the institution of marriage. As suggested earlier, thinking about marriage is a different thing—from personal experience I would say a vastly different thing—from thinking like a married person. Perhaps by now that is obvious. But when it comes to thinking like a married person there exists within this perspective different levels of what might be called thinking institutionally. You and I both might work on our particular marriage relationships quite faithfully, really trying to do what it takes to sustain and develop the relationships with our respective spouses. But it is in addressing the question of "why" we are ultimately making this effort that the different levels of institutional thinking start coming into view.

I work on the relationship with my spouse (communication, respect, task-sharing, and the whole litany of being a good partner) because I know that if this relationship is working, things will go better for me. I am at the Doctor Phil level of things, the calculative level of knowing that "if Mama ain't happy, ain't nobody happy." And at one level this view makes obvious sense. But it also bespeaks a wholly contingent loyalty to the relationship and behind that, to the institution of marriage. If trying to make Mamma happy doesn't eventually make things go better for me in this relationship, then, well, it is time to head for the exit. In effect, I have deconstructed the notion of fidelity to the point where it simply means my faithfulness to me.

You, on the other hand, are working on the relationship with your spouse as I am, but with a deeper commitment to honoring the marriage institution itself. Because you do not believe that an unrewarding marriage should simply be jettisoned, you are more willing to invest time and effort in your marriage than I am in mine. You will make many more attempts than I do to resolve marital disagreements. You will find your own dissatisfaction an insufficient cause simply to give up on the marriage. While I am "working on the relationship," you on the other hand are laboring over it in a much more self-sacrificing way. The differing results should come as no surprise, although it does seem to come as a surprise to social scientists. In the long run, my greater sense of freedom to leave an unsatisfying marriage increases the likelihood that my marriage will become unsatisfying and something to be left behind.[26]

Obviously, everything depends on whether the partners entered into a marriage have compatible expectations. If both see their relationship as a conditional contract of mutual convenience, the longevity of their arrangement may be relatively short, but the psychological costs of abandoning the marriage should be small (that is in theory; in practice, the costs in various categories are rarely small). By the same token, if both partners see marriage as a covenantal, rather than contractual, commitment of life together until death strikes, the psychological burden of abandoning this shared identity will be huge and the marriage likely to be long-lasting. (The practical implication is, if you are thinking institutionally about marriage, avoid someone who is not; and if you are not thinking in that way, avoid someone who is. Life will proceed much more smoothly, though perhaps not more meaningfully.) If marriage or any other institution is to be sustained through the vicissitudes of time and circumstance, the support has to be based more on what people are willing to put into it than on what they are currently getting out of it. Such willingness to invest is a hallmark of thinking institutionally.

In all of this there is an important message. It is especially important for those who have been lured into thinking that the true value of something consists simply in the fact that I, the creator of my life as a work of art, have chosen it. This message is saying something to the contrary and well worth considering. The infusion of value means that thinking institutionally is not a matter of personal whim, as if you get out of bed and decide that today I will think this way. And it is certainly not a question of following a six-step IDEALS program for critical thinking. To be institutionally minded is to enter and participate in a world of larger, self-transcendent meanings. On a grand scale, the self-transcendent reference may involve some profound cultural ideal, or sense of historic purpose, or religious understanding of what God expects of human beings. Or the self-transcendent meaning may be something in the middle distance, such as a professional calling, family business, artistic tradition, or community identity.

Whatever the case, because institutions are an inheritance of valued purpose and moral obligation, they constitute socially ordered groundings for human life. Such grounding in a normative field implicates the lives of individuals and collectivities in a lived-out social reality. That is a far different thing from pursuit of the socially disembodied ideal. Those pursuing the undefined, institutionally ungrounded ideal seek to bring down to earth the abstractions of social justice, nationhood, holy truth, and the like. It is the lure of utopianism. Because they are respectful of what has been delivered and attentive to the strong evaluations that serve as guides in a disoriented world, persons thinking institutionally are in a good position to perceive the horror that lies behind utopianism's alluring smile. They can see the dangers posed to both collectivities and individuals. Dreams of the institutionless, abstract ideal have left human beings vulnerable to the yearning for total revolution, from the French Revolution onward through communism, fascism, and Maoism. The cost of pursuing the collective dream is well over a hundred million lives cut short in the century just past.

The dream of a life without institutions in pursuit of the undefined ideal also occurs at the individual level. Here the total revolution promises that each person can be the artistic creator of his or her own meaning of life. At this level too the institutionalist is well positioned to recognize the danger. This danger is the tendency for institutionally ungrounded commitments to self-expression to slide over into self-indulgence and, from there, to ultimate self-destruction. In intellectual circles and popular culture alike, celebrity stars glamorize a life without institutions, and many fans seem to enjoy living vicariously through the personal anarchy of a Michel Foucault, Timothy Leary, Janice Joplin, or Kurt Cobain. What others see as a heroic turning of one's life into an autonomous work of art, the institutionalist sees as misguided foolishness and likely to turn into a work of self-immolation.

Thus, with its socially and historically grounded infusions of value, the natural effect of institutional thinking is to pull down the utopian. But its natural effect is also to lift up the mundane work of ordinary life to something more in keeping with the human spirit. In Chapter 2 we reviewed a litany of misdeeds in the public, private, and nonprofit sectors, and such scandals involving prominent people and organizations naturally attract our attention. But in going about our daily lives we are often scandalized in another kind of way. For example, we encounter the store attendant who is not attending to much of anything, especially the customer. Or it is a coworker who is working at everything except the task at hand. Or it might be the slacker student or the slacker teacher who is merely going through the motions of the day's lesson plan. What these big and little scandals all have in common amounts to this: people not doing the job that is supposed to be done.

Being institutionally minded will certainly not eliminate such common annoyances. But it does put us in a position to honor the mundane activities of daily life more than we might otherwise do. It helps us to appreciate the importance of taking responsibility for doing the job right in some larger institutional scheme of things. It helps us to realize that people who fail us institutionally are not just making miscalculations or errors in doing something. They are failing at being something they are supposed to be. Whether a doctor, teacher, plumber, computer programmer, checkout clerk, janitor, or preacher—we all make mistakes in our jobs under a variety of circumstances. It is

another thing to willfully violate the very point of beir
tor, teacher, plumber, computer programmer, janitor, or
The former is a conditional miscalculation or misundei
The latter is a betrayal of position and ultimately of being.

Institutional Thinking as a Stretching
of Time Horizons

It follows from earlier points that institutional thinking also
involves being mindful about time in a particular way. To think
institutionally is to stretch your time horizon backward and forward so that the shadows from both past and future lengthen
into the present. Earlier, we saw how this takes the form of
receiving and handling carefully what has been delivered from
the past. In this section we want to look more broadly at the
time horizons of institutional thinking in linking past and
future. As we will see, just because a person is thinking about the
future does not mean he or she is thinking institutionally.

To think institutionally is to be attentive to precedent.
Unfortunately, to modern ears that evokes an image of being
controlled by the "dead hand of the past." A more adequate view
of institutional thinking understands precedent as a form of solidarity. Choices made in the present serve to strengthen or erode
solidarity among an "us" that is peopled by the living, the dead,
and the yet unborn. Because there are attachments through
time, institutional thinking means living an implicated life,
always both inheriting and bequeathing. As the poet John
Donne put it, it is to see yourself as "at once receiver and the
legacy."[27]

A sense of this perspective might be gained if you imagine
having a time portal in your room. Through this portal step people of your society from times past and times future. Meeting
those coming from the past, you hear questions like this: What
have you done with what we have freely given to you? Are you
mindful of it? What is the evidence that you are taking good
care of it in your times? Is there gratitude in your work? And

then there come people from the future stepping through the portal to have a word with you. From them you hear questions like this: Why didn't you pass on to us in better order the things you received? What lack of care for us caused you to saddle us with your debts rather than provide us the advantage of your investments? Have you cherished yourself over us? Is there respect for us in your work?

Granted, my poor takeoff on Dickens's *Christmas Carol* may be too fanciful, but it is trying to make an important point. When thinking institutionally, current decisions are made with a continuing awareness that you are enjoying the fruits of something belonging to predecessors and successors. Therefore, while change is inevitable, the recognition of its implications is embedded in a strong appreciation for what has gone on before you were here and what will go on after you are gone. That is the broad understanding of precedent, and it is something far different from being under remote control by the cold, dead hand of the past. On the contrary. A sense of inheritance backward and forward in time can always keep finding fresh work for such stewardship. To put it another way, institutional thinking shapes conduct by making it beholden to its own past history and to the history it is creating. The present is never only the present. It is one moment in a going concern. And that going concern makes a strong claim on not only one's decisions and actions but also one's affections. It is like receiving and passing on a kiss through a veil.

To be constrained in the present by partaking of the fruits of what belongs to predecessors and successors has a venerable legal name, so venerable that it is traceable back to pre-Christian Roman law. The term is "usufruct." It refers to the right to make full use of something while also being under the obligation to pass on intact, without injury, the substance of the thing itself. It is the tenant's right to enjoy as well as the tenant's responsibility to protect an asset belonging to others. Pick and profit from the fruit of the orchard, but make sure the orchard's trees are there for the next tenants to enjoy.

Usufruct is a fruitful concept for considering the stretching of time horizons that is entailed in thinking institutionally. At first glance, it might seem that we need to do no more than invoke this idea and we have neatly defined one of the characteristics of being institutionally minded. But we need to think again. To be thinking about the future and the right of usufruct is by no means necessarily the same thing as to be thinking institutionally. To see why, we can turn to an exchange of letters on the issue of usufruct. The letters were sent between two friends who also happened to possess two of the best minds that have ever graced American public life. The differing viewpoints expressed in these letters between Thomas Jefferson and James Madison take us to the heart of the matter and will repay careful consideration.

A Tale of Two Letters

Thomas Jefferson had left Monticello for France to be the ambassador to America's indispensable ally in the recent war against Britain. On September 9, 1789, he wrote to his friend and Virginia neighbor James Madison about a novel idea he had. The intellectual and political context for this idea is crucially important. It had been prompted by the intellectual conversations swirling in France about the elemental, self-evident principles of political society.

During the four months before Jefferson put pen to paper, King Louis XVI had convened the Estates-General for the first time in 175 years; the Third Estate, claiming to represent the nation, had broken with the Estates of the clergy and nobility to form the National Assembly and man top government positions; Paris mobs had stormed the Bastille and rural mobs had threatened landlords; the National Assembly had issued decrees nullifying peasants' ancient feudal obligations, and then followed that up at the end of August by issuing "The Declaration of the Rights of Man and the Citizen." At least on paper, a nation of equal citizens under the law would now be the sovereign power in France. In a mere one summer, centuries-old institutions of France's ancien régime had crumbled. Jefferson was writing toward the end of what we now know was only the first stage of the horrific French Revolution. A whole institutional infrastructure was being destroyed, and in its place—the undefined ideals of liberty, equality, and fraternity. They were the anti-institutional and socially disembodied claims for power that anyone could and did use for personal purposes in the years ahead.

For his part, James Madison in 1789 had left his home at Montpelier for Philadelphia to take a leading role in the First Congress created by America's new Constitution. In those same four months before Jefferson wrote his letter on usufruct, Madison had been active in the first session of this First Congress, enacting laws that created the administrative institutions for the new national government—departments of State, War, Treasury, the Office of Attorney General, and a system of national courts. More than that, in this four-month period Madison almost single-handedly won congressional passage of the amendments to the Constitution that we now call the Bill of Rights.[28] And yet a little over a year earlier Madison had consistently opposed adding amendments for a Bill of Rights to the proposed Constitution. Knowing a little more about this context will help us to understand the letter Madison eventually sent back to Jefferson.[29]

Madison's inconsistency is only on the surface, and it was something much more than political expediency. His opposition to and then championing of a Bill of Rights actually expressed an underlying consistency—a consistency in thinking institutionally—about the new Constitution. Here is why.

For Madison and those of his generation supporting the American Revolution, the underlying aspiration was for a system of self-government by free men. With a military revolution won in 1781, the question for practical reasoning was how to make that ultimate goal possible. After six years of disillusionment and disorder, the eventual institutional answer proposed to the people in 1787 was a Constitution as best the Founders (heavily influenced by Madison) could design it. That answer proposed to create a truly national government with powers that were limited but necessary for being a single nation. The issue would then be how to begin institutionalizing the Constitution's answer so as to make such a design keep going through time. Thinking constitutionally is raising thinking institutionally to the nth power. And in the transition between the drafting of the Constitution in 1787 and its first months of operation in 1789, that is what James Madison was doing.

Madison originally opposed adding a Bill of Rights on several grounds. He and others argued that it was unnecessary. Since the national government would have only specifically enumerated powers, there was no need for amendments saying that it could not do what it had no power to do. Moreover, listing rights could be taken to mean that unlisted rights did not exist and could create an illusion of security behind mere "parchment barriers." Not least of all, allowing state ratification on condition that certain amendments be added was equivalent to allowing the opponents of a strong national government to destroy the Constitution's design. Thus Madison and his allies stood firm on the principle required if the design itself were not to be strangled at birth. State ratifying conventions had to vote the proposed Constitution up or down, without amendment.

However, at the ratifying conventions in crucial states, it became clear to Madison that without assurances that amendments would be forthcoming in the future, there might well be no birth for the Constitution in the first place. Thus ratification finally and narrowly occurred in Massachusetts, and above all Virginia, on the understanding that once the new government was in place, amendments suggested by the state conventions would be appropriately considered. By making that bargain, Madison accomplished something important. Since proposed changes would now occur within the Constitution's own design for amending itself, any such changes would be a step helping to institutionalize that very design.

So it was that on the day in May when Louis XVI reluctantly convened the Estates-General, Madison stood up in the

House of Representatives to make an announcement. He would shortly introduce a package of proposed amendments to the Constitution. Pouring over the nearly two hundred amendments that had been suggested in the state ratification debates, Madison eventually distilled a list of nine that he laid before Congress in June. Excluded were all those amendments that would have changed the Constitution's institutional structures and powers. Retained and summarized were mainly those proposed amendments pertaining to personal liberties.

Protected from amendments that sought to change and likely destroy the Constitution's institutional design (that is, a truly national government of limited but strong powers), amending the Constitution to add a Bill of Rights could now plausibly be seen in a new light. Madison's proposed amendments would not only be keeping faith with the understandings given at state ratifying conventions. They would also strengthen the Constitution by deepening and broadening its public support. The state ratifying conventions had made the popular concern about protecting rights very clear. In Madison's words, the new Bill of Rights would help "extinguish from the bosom of every member of the community any apprehensions, that there are those among his countrymen who wish to deprive them of the liberty for which they valiantly fought and honorably bled." In other words, the Constitution would be further institutionalized by a Bill of Rights tying the document to the nation's Revolutionary history and founding goal of liberty.

The demands of political expediency would have been met by mere proposals. However, Madison kept faith with the unwritten constitutional process that had brought things to this point. He not only proposed but also worked tirelessly and almost single-handedly to gain congressional approval, even when legislative bargaining eliminated the amendment he most favored (one that would have prohibited the states, and not only the federal government, from violating individual rights). At the end of September, Congress finally passed twelve amendments to the Constitution and sent them to the states for ratification.

The Argument

With this background we are better prepared to hear what Jefferson and Madison are saying, not just to each other but also to us. Their contrasting voices can help us understand the difference between institutional thinking and its opposite when it comes to looking toward the future in light of the past. So now at last we come to the letters.

Jefferson's idea, which he thought had "never to have been started either on this or our side of the water" was as follows. The essential question is whether one generation has a right to bind another generation. Jefferson's answer is that no such obligation can rightfully be transmitted through time. "I set out on this ground which I suppose to be self-evident, 'that the earth belongs in usufruct to the living'; that the dead have neither powers nor rights over it." Jefferson begins by considering the natural right of the individual. Of course, under the laws of a society there can be rules for the transfer of property to descendants, but the question here is not about social conventions. It is about the abstract natural right of individuals, and here, Jefferson argues, the situation is clear.

> The portion [of the earth] occupied by any individual ceases to be his when himself ceases to be, and reverts to the society…no man can by *natural right* oblige the lands he occupied, or the persons who succeed him in that occupation to the payment of debts contracted by him. For if he could, he might during his own life eat up the usufruct of the lands for several generations to come, and then the lands would belong to the dead, and not to the living, which would be reverse of our principle.

Jefferson then goes on to extend the same principle to the societal level. "What is true of every member of the society individually is true of the all collectively, since the rights of the whole can be no more than the sum of the rights of individuals." He makes this extension of principle possible by conceptualizing society in terms of individual generations. He first imagines a society of succeeding generations where each generation is born on the same day, reaches maturity at age twenty-one, and dies at age fifty-five (then the current life expectancy at age twenty-one). In effect, when a generation leaves the stage at a fixed moment "as individuals do now," the whole society dies and is replaced by the next generation.

The point of Jefferson's thought experiment is to show that, as with individuals, "the earth belongs to each of these generations during its course, fully, and in their own right." If the first generation could charge the second with its debt, the second charge the third with its debt, and so on, "then the earth would not belong to the living." Thus no generation can rightfully contract obligatory arrangements beyond the course of its own existence. At age twenty-one the generation may bind itself for thirty-four years; at age fifty-four for only one year.

Of course, Jefferson acknowledges that the timing is not as neat as this, with a generation undergoing "a constant course of decay and renewal." But in Jefferson's way of thinking the problem is a purely mechanical one of timing and easily overcome by consulting the mortality tables. Doing so shows that "generations changing daily, by daily deaths and births, have one constant term beginning at the date of their contract and ending when a majority of those of full age at that date [of contract] shall be dead." It turns out that those of an age (that is, twenty-one or older) to form a majority will be dead in roughly nineteen years. It follows that since the will of the majority binds the whole, "19 years is the term beyond which neither the representatives of a nation, nor even the whole nation itself assembled, can validly extend a debt."

However, debt is only one example of obligation that a generation may transmit to the future. Jefferson pursues the logic to its end, such that the validity of every act of society is limited to nineteen years.

> On similar ground it may be proved that no society can make a perpetual constitution, or even a perpetual law. The earth belongs

always to the living generation. They may manage it then, and what proceeds from it, as they please, during their usufruct. They are masters too of their own persons, and, consequently, may govern them as they please. But persons and property make the sum of the objects of government. The constitution and the laws of their predecessors extinguished then, in their natural course, with those whose will gave them being. This could preserve that being till it ceased to be itself, and no longer. Every constitution, then, and every law naturally expires at the end of 19 years. If it be enforced longer, it is an act of force and not of right.

For Jefferson, the fact that the next generation could obviously repeal any constitution or law if it chose to do so was insufficient. The practical difficulties in organizing any such repeal meant implicitly that the arrangements carried forward from the past would remain in force. Only an explicit, fixed term of one generation for all acts of society would satisfy the requirement for an express declaration of the public will, so that no generation will be binding another.

These were not idle speculations on Jefferson's part. He closed his letter by urging Madison to raise this idea in the new government and to include it in the preamble to the first national law for raising revenue. Even thirty-five years later, Jefferson was still writing to his correspondents on this theme. "We may consider each generation as a distinct nation, with a right, by the will of its majority, to bind themselves, but none to bind the succeeding generation, more than the inhabitants of another country."[30]

What is Madison to say? If you have overseen the creation and protection of the Constitution's design, helped erect the first national administrative structure of government, and made the Bill of Rights a legislative reality binding the Constitution to America's revolutionary cause, what do you say about the idea that all of this should have a nineteen-year expiration date and then, if everyone in the next generation would prefer, simply start all over again?

What Madison says is respectful, intellectually penetrating, and a fine expositive example of thinking institutionally. He does not begin with the abstract individual, a concept so attractive to Jefferson and the leading minds of the French Revolution, as well as to Rousseau earlier. Indeed, that is why Rousseau could look at swaddling clothes and coffins and miss the whole point. By contrast, Madison begins with the concept of law. He suggests to Jefferson that the acts of a political society can be divided into three types of law: the fundamental law of the constitution, the laws stipulating that they cannot be revoked at the will of the legislature, and all other laws lacking that irrevocable quality. And so, from his institutional way of thinking, Madison begins the work of demolishing Jefferson's idea.

As for the fundamental law of the constitution, Madison argues that the problem lies in applying Jefferson's theoretical scheme to the real world. First, a constitutional order ceasing at the end of a given term would "be too subject to the casualty and consequences of an interregnum." In other words, disorderly dead zones would be created in the life of the nation. These would be periods devoid of any institutional connections as our political society transitioned from the prior regime to the next expressly chosen regime. Second, a constitutional government subject to expiration dates would "become too mutable and novel to retain that share of prejudice in its favor which is a salutary aid to the most rational government." In other words, Jefferson's idea would not allow for the development through time of the patriotic emotional attachments that even the most well-thought-out constitutional design needs in order to be sustained. Third, the anticipation of a periodic open season for total revision of the constitutional order would generate confusion in the public's mind and incentives for powerful, self-seeking groups to exploit such confusions to their own selfish purposes.

In short, from his institutionalist perspective, Madison is politely saying that Jefferson's idea of a constitutional order is no constitutional order at all. It is a repeated throw of the historical dice, offering each generation the chance to bet the house on something new.

Madison then turns to the second type of laws, those involving "stipulations" that prevent their revocation by the mere will of the majority in a legislature. Here he undermines Jefferson's idea by going to its roots and examining what I have called the institutional notion of "taking delivery." Madison asks, "If the earth be the gift of nature to the living, their title can extend to the earth in its *natural* state only. The *improvements* made by the dead form a debt against the living who take the benefit of them. This debt cannot be otherwise discharged than by a proportionate obedience to the will of the authors of the improvements." Again, in a very polite way, Madison is saying that Jefferson has misunderstood the way in which human beings exist. They are not a succession of lone figures occupying a piece of physical nature in space-time. They are social creatures inheriting everything that their fellow social creatures have made of the physical world and passed on to them.

Madison next shifts the focus forward in time and again undercuts Jefferson's narrow, abstractly individualistic view of obligation. "Debts may be incurred with a direct view to the interests of the unborn as well as the living." For example, the debts involved in protecting our nation from foreign aggressors will benefit untold future generations. Madison's implied question is: Should we stop defending the nation when the war debt exceeds what can be repaid in the next nineteen years? Likewise, debts may be incurred primarily for the benefit of the next and later generations. Here Madison's implied question is: Should we not invest in any future beyond the nineteen-year end of our own generation's nose? For this second kind of law, Madison concludes, "There seems, then, to be some foundation in the nature of things, in the relation which one generation bears to another, for the *descent* of obligations from one [generation] to another. Equity may require it. Mutual good may be promoted by it. And all that seems indispensable in stating the account between the dead and the living is to see that the debts against the latter do not exceed the advances made by the former."

Thus in place of Jefferson's mechanical and abstract logic, Madison leaves it as a matter of making an inherently historical, socially attentive judgment. We the living must decide if we are violating an intergenerational trust by burdening others with more than we received from the past. That, of course, is an impossible calculation, but Madison is not calling for an accountant's calculation. He is asking that a self-governing people stretch their time horizons and in that light of intergenerational responsibility, seriously think about what they are doing.

Madison then turns to the third category of law, the mass of ordinary laws that are freely made and unmade at the will of the legislature. Here the problems with Jefferson's idea are "merely practical" but no less devastating. Such ordinary laws establish a web of rights and obligations between parties, especially regarding property. Operation of these laws would now sink into a morass of violent struggles as parties jockeyed for advantage amid the uncertainty generated by periodic expiration of the larger constitutional and legal order. But it would not be an equal struggle. Now the burden of difficulty in organizing a successful repeal would shift to those wanting to renew the status quo after nineteen years. It is "anarchy" that would now be advantaged, and Madison spells out how. By weakening people's sense of "all the obligations dependent on antecedent laws and usages," the frequent return of periods superseding such obligations would inevitably:

- undermine the value of property rights, especially as expiration periods approached;
- encourage selfish attitudes of licentiousness that are already too powerful in people;
- discourage all efforts at steady industry pursued under the sanction of existing laws; and
- give immediate advantage to the clever and shrewd over other parts of society.

Madison concludes by showing that the problems with Jefferson's idea stem from thinking that only express consent to a regime of government and laws can render them legitimate. Seeing institutions embodied in relationships ongoing through time, Madison insists that "a tacit assent may be given to established governments and laws, and that this assent is to be inferred from the omission of an express revocation." That has to be so if the political society is to be able to function.

To show this Madison asks, "On what principle is it that the voice of the majority binds the minority?" It is a seemingly innocent question, but it cuts to the heart of Jefferson's endorsement of a social-political order based solely on the natural right of each generation. It asks, What is the principle of natural right by which a majority binds a minority of any given generation? The answer is that there is no such principle in the law of nature. The rule for deciding by the majority voice has been one principle among others that has been found useful in political society, just as on some issues, such as creating and changing a constitution, a rule requiring decision by something much greater than a mere majority may be useful. Here we should let Madison finish the argument in his own words. Prior to the instituting of such useful majority-decision rules:

> *unanimity* was necessary; and rigid theory accordingly presupposes the assent of every individual to the rule which subjects the minority to the will of the majority. If this assent cannot be given tacitly, or be not implied where no positive evidence forbids, no person born in society could, on attaining ripe age [that is, twenty-one], be bound by any acts of the majority, and either a unanimous renewal of every law would be necessary as often as a new member should be added to the society, or the express consent of every new member be obtained to the rule by which the majority decides for the whole.

In his letter to Jefferson, Madison respectfully leaves it as a question, but the answer to the question is clear. Jefferson's idea would subvert "the very foundation of civil society."[31]

Raising Our Sights

Clearly, Thomas Jefferson had a vivid sense of usufruct, to the point of claiming the sovereignty of each living generation and the nonexistent rights of any other. People who do not exist, he said, cannot have rights. He saw the situation, not in terms of obligations one generation might owe to another, but in terms of what any living generation must not do to the next. It must not impose any law, constitution, or other binding obligation. Like today's professors of postmodern cultural criticism, Jefferson viewed the influence of the past as solely an oppressive force. His thinking was tuned to what I described earlier as "the undefined ideal" abstracted from the institutions and historical ligatures of society.

Jefferson never gave any sign of seriously engaging Madison's powerful and institutionally informed arguments against his idea. For decades he was content simply to keep repeating his abstract notion of the natural right of each generation to be a "different nation" from the others. By contrast, James Madison understood political society as a going concern. Its generations were not by right different nations. As a social and historical fact, the generations were participants in a great chain letter that was being handled, amended, and passed down through time. The constitutional order and system of laws were instruments making possible the generations'—a people's—joint venture together, and these instruments were carried forward through tacit assent. The ties of moral obligation between past, present, and future were inescapable if a political society were to succeed as a going concern.[32]

In 1790, Madison seemed to catch only a glimpse of the idea of the Union. It lay like a sprouting seed in the year-old Constitution. Even so, he had a glimpse and objected to Jefferson's idea of stopping and restarting a constitutional regime every nineteen years. As he asked rhetorically, would not such a government "become too mutable and novel to retain that share of prejudice in its favor which is a salutary aid to the most rational government?" By the early 1830s, as the last survivor among the Constitution's drafters, Madison had more than a glimpse of what was at stake. He struggled to oppose the growing doctrine of state nullification of national law, a doctrine that would destroy the American Union as defined by the Constitution. Before dying in 1836 his last message to the current generation gave advice that was "nearest to my heart and deepest in my convictions, . . . *that the union of the states be cherished and perpetuated.*" The substantive identity of a people had been institutionalized in the Constitution. For this people, the Union expressed in the Constitution was the indispensable instrument for their republican ideals of self-government.[33]

Another generation more and, faced with the ultimate crisis, Abraham Lincoln could articulate the vision as none had before. It was a vision of solidarity across all generations of Americans, with the Constitution as their institution of Union, aspiring to the republican ideals of liberty and equality. In his first inaugural address he called it the people's "mystic chord of memory." America was not a contractual union of individuals in the present generation, any more than it was a mere group of states contracting to create a friendship league for safety and convenience. Entering or leaving a contract changes nothing of substance. Entering a covenant changes your identity, and leaving a covenant is of devastating consequence for that identity. Lincoln's way of thinking, like Madison's, was everything that Jefferson's was not. Lincoln and Madison thought institutionally about the life of the nation. For Jefferson, there was no such thing—only the life of each passing individual and generation. Lincoln gave elegant expression to what was implicit in Madison's tightly reasoned letter and explicit in his fight to pass the Bill of Rights. Lincoln fused the ideals of the Declaration of Independence, the institution of the Constitution, and the shared history of the nation, invoking each generation's covenantal solidarity with ancestors and posterity, a union organic and even sacramental.[34]

Now, in a roundabout but, I hope, better informed way, we can at last return to the third of our "rational choice" cases. It is the one left unaddressed in Chapter 3 after we considered the Law Merchant and king's power cases in relation to George Washington's performance in thinking institutionally. You may recall that the specific subject matter of this third and most difficult case concerns economic transaction costs and the inescapable need for some authority empowered to enforce rules of the game. These are the rules that are necessary if any mutually beneficial exchanges are to be a realistic possibility. The general problem is that any ruler with sufficient power to enforce the needed rules for the common good will also be powerful enough to enforce rules serving only his own good. And why, rationally speaking, would a ruler not do so?

To have their work accepted, the Framers of the U.S. Constitution essentially had to satisfy the challenge posed by that question. Amid widespread perceptions of domestic turmoil threatening property rights, commerce, and the rule of law itself, they were proposing to empower a new national government that would create and enforce the needed rules. But why should the people agree to bind themselves under such an authority when it could just as well rule in its own interest and against their liberties?

Obviously, there is no room here to follow all the intricate arguments and developments that led to acceptance of the U.S. Constitution as the supreme law of the land. The advocates gave assurances that the new government was not a ruler but a reflection of the people's self-rule. They promised that republican liberties would be safeguarded by the Constitution's very design (that is, a government limited to the powers enumerated, with internal checks and balances among three branches, with external checks and balances of federalism in relation to the states, and with the promise of a bill of rights). But why take a leap of faith into such assurances and promises? What accounts for not only ratification but also the ongoing tacit assent to the constitutional order that was crucial during those first troubled decades of national life? Read through the history of this remarkable period—say, the thirty years from 1772 to 1802—

and you are left repeatedly asking yourself, How in the world did these people pull off such a thing?

Of course, there can be many explanations, but it is no help simply to say that enough people decided to act rationally in their long-term self-interest. You are not likely to act in your long-term interests unless you are first thinking about your interests in a long-term way. I believe the evidence shows that behind the myriad arguments, there was constant recourse to a particular outlook, an appreciative stance, that had been shaped during the events of that generation. It was a triad of thoughts amounting to one grand theme, and it recurs throughout all the disputes and potential turning points. In fact, it is repeated so many times in so many quarters and varying ways that after a while one almost stops noticing it.

First, there is the notion that mankind's ancient hopes for freedom have been handed down to this generation of the American Revolution. The Greek and Roman classics, Bible stories, the rise and fall of the Dutch Republic, and above all, the centuries of struggles for the rights of Englishmen all spoke to this notion.

Second, a great many Americans were convinced that there was a larger meaning to their actions and the events of their time. What was happening was a momentous experiment testing whether or not republican self-government could work.

Third, Americans were convinced that, one way or the other, the results of their experiment would reverberate into the distant future—to all "posterity," as they often called it.

Because this tripartite formulation became such a familiar way of interpreting events does not mean that it should be dismissed as rhetorical window dressing. On the contrary, it means that we should take it very seriously as a force in those times. There is good evidence that many Americans of different social stations considered themselves engaged in a portentous joint venture and shared a genuine, continuing fear that it would fail.[35] Preserving the republican experiment meant saving not only Congress from the states or the states from each other but especially the people from themselves. Supporters of the Constitutional order were having to convince the ruler—the people—to constrain himself with a Constitution that greatly restricted the majoritarian premises of popular government itself. To accept and continue supporting that arrangement, people needed some larger way of thinking about specific goals and actions of the day.

The thought triad just sketched did that. It spurred some critical mass of people in this generation to be involved in the three features of what I have called thinking institutionally. Such people realized that they had taken delivery of something of immense importance, the hope of the ages for human freedom and equal rights. They saw their political work infused with value going well beyond the controversies of the moment; the aspiration for self-government itself was on trial. And they saw the stakes of their work stretching forward to untold future generations all around the world—or, as the aged Madison put it, "the last hope of true liberty on the face of the Earth." Their work in thinking institutionally was not beyond partisanship, but it was well beyond ordinary, shortsighted pursuit of partisan payoffs.[36] What they had received as heritage, they did indeed take as task and thus made it their own.

There was nothing inevitable about the acceptance of the Constitution or its initial survival. It was touch and go all the way. And the fault lines did not run so much between different people as between different parts of people's minds. They ran between thinking in an institutional way and thinking in a narrower, short-term, self-indulgent way. They also ran between thinking in an institutional way and thinking in the abstract, socially disembodied way of the undefined ideal.

★ ★ ★

Of course, all this was a long time ago. Today we are caught up in talk about institutions failing us. But look closely and I think you will see that when institutions fail, it is mainly a matter of people failing institutions. People fail institutions by failing to think and act with due regard to the valued purposes embodied in institutions. To repeat an earlier point, the failure does not consist in simply making mistakes, errors, and miscalculations. It consists in failures of being.

Consider again the lists in Chapter 2's cavalcade of misconduct that occurred throughout the public, private, and nonprofit realms in the last half-century. Ask yourself, what is it that really failed?

Just suppose that the leading figures involved in any of these events had resisted temptations to the contrary and had actually held fast to the idea of behaving in an institutionally appropriate way. Suppose that these people from yesterday's headlines had been of a mind to think that their private, personal agendas were something to be subordinated to their institutional responsibilities. Suppose they had been of a mind to weigh the moral claims of the past and their obligations to the future and had viewed their choices about how to act in that light. Perhaps not all, but certainly the vast majority of items on those lists would be blotted out. And how much better off would everyone have been as a result.

As I suggested in Chapter 2, there is more to thinking institutionally than just being extra careful to avoid breaking the rules, much less being clever enough to avoid criminal indictment. It entails entering into the spirit of things, and by the end of this chapter I hope you have a better sense of what that might mean. Amid the perpetual perishing that marks our individual existences, institutions are weathered presences. It is intellectually interesting and important to think about them. But it is more humanly valuable to enter into the way of thinking that they embody—in other words, to seek and place value on their interior point of view.

It may sound like I am saying that thinking institutionally is all about being unselfish, rationally uncalculating, and altruistic—indeed bordering on the saintly. That is not so. But since institutional thinking is always pointing to something beyond the self-life, it naturally can appear to onlookers as a matter of self-denial rather than self-assertion. But thinking institutionally is, in its own way, a kind of self-assertion. It asserts not a negation of self but a giving of self.

To borrow language from another context, thinking institutionally is a sign or a witness: it alone does not say everything, but rather grows by saying what it is not and revealing what it points to.[37]

Institutional thinking resists utopianism in projects of both social construction and self-construction. But it also insists that mundane life is far more than a banal submission to expediency. It views the present as thoroughly enriched by inheritance and legacy. Again, to borrow a thought from a religious context, thinking institutionally tends to humble without humiliating us, to raise us up without flattering us.

CHAPTER FIVE
APPLICATIONS, DANGERS,
AND THE UPHILL JOURNEY

Since it is always possible to think without acting, thinking institutionally does not necessarily translate into acting institutionally. Without deeds, an "institutionally minded appreciative stance" is frankly rather pointless (in addition to being bad writing).

That obvious fact does not need to be belabored, but it is certainly worth keeping in mind. The subject we are dealing with is meant to be "practical" in the classic sense—directed to action. Without people thinking institutionally and then acting institutionally to make them real, institutions truly are little more than the unpopulated, empty formalities that extreme behaviorialists dismiss. No one really lives there. The firm, the legislative body, the university, the profession, the marriage, and the family—all such institutions then merely become sites for fleeting, self-centered transactions with no deeper and more enduring meanings. To repeat, the point in these later chapters is not to think *about* institutions. It is to engage an interior point of view where thinking institutionally is a means of orientation to a world in which one is *participating*. Thinking institutionally, you do not "experience" the institution. There is not that remoteness. You stand in full relation to the institution and its values. It is what your deeds actualize.

What is it to act institutionally? What does the deed look like? The last chapter, in passing, gave a few examples from the hard sciences, law, marriage, and the persons of George Washington and James Madison. In this chapter we will look at some more familiar examples from everyday life. Then we will consider the negative implications of institutional thinking. What about slavery and other "bad" institutions? Finally, we will try to face up to some hard truths about why it is now so difficult to find the intellectual and moral resources for thinking and acting institutionally. Why must it be such an uphill struggle?

Profession, Office, Stewardship

What does institutional thinking look like when it is translated into action? It is more common than you might think, but to see it requires taking our eyes off foreground features and vigorously focusing on the background. There we can witness the presumptions about rightful relationships being played out, or not played out. What we are watching are enactments involving trust in identity amid assumptions of institutional purpose. That abstract statement may not seem to mean much. So let us take an experience that has no doubt been shared by everyone.

Imagine walking into a high school or college classroom on the first day of school. In the foreground is the usual gossiping back and forth with students you already know, the awkward meeting with people you do not know, and the fussing about to find seats in light of those social facts of life. And there are the first glances between teacher and students before class begins, each taking a preliminary measure of the other. What I would like us to focus on are the assumptions in the background of this situation on that first day, the presuppositions in play as a group of strangers gradually begins unfolding into a class composed of teacher and students. What are you taking for granted?

Among many other things (for example, that class will be taught in English, that it will continue for a fixed period of time each week, and so on), you are assuming that your teachers are who they say they are. But pause and consider—the person standing in front of the room who is beginning to speak will in all likelihood do no more than give his or her name and not make explicit claims about who he or she is or how he or she comes to be here speaking to you. Without trying to demonstrate or prove anything to you, this person in the front of the classroom is taking on the authority of a teacher and you are taking up the role of a student. Neither of you has sought to discuss who you are in order to be doing what you are doing. Nor will you ever discuss it. You will simply start doing it.

However, the assumption in this background goes deeper than presuming "this is my teacher." It goes to the notion that my teacher and any teacher is "something," a person with a particular competence and purpose. For example, you would be surprised if I told you that the person in the front of your classroom is your teacher because he or she did personal favors for the chairman of the school board, or bribed someone in the Ministry of Education, or was the cousin of your school's principal. Likewise you would be surprised to hear that the grade you receive will depend on the amount of money and gifts you send your teacher's way. Moreover, the subjects you will be studying are a confection of half-baked ideas some political patron in the Ministry of Education has developed, and no one really cares if you come to class, as long as you pay your school fees. You would not just be surprised. You would say that something is wrong here, meaning roughly "things are not in their proper order."

It will not do to say that it is a bureaucracy or some educational apparatus that one is taking for granted to regulate the school system. A well-organized, fairly efficient bureaucracy could be readily devoted to the processing of false certifications for teachers, managing a patronage-based curriculum, and policing the proper payoffs from students to teachers for grades. If you join the Peace Corps or otherwise travel to teach in many parts of the non-Western world, these are the kinds of things you can expect to encounter in the classroom.

What you know is "wrong" about the imaginary situation I have presented is that it is out of keeping with the purpose of having a classroom, students, and a teacher standing in front of the room in the first place. It is missing "the point" of it all. In recognizing that, what you are taking for granted is an institutional order—meaning that people should think and act in ways appropriate to the purposes of that order. However much you might dislike a particular teacher, the subject matter, or anything else about the class, in sitting down in the classroom that first day you were participating, through your unspoken expectations, in the enactment of that order. However "institutionalized" any patronage, bribery, social favoritism, and so on might be, you understand implicitly that these things would be a perverted, parasitic version of the right order of things. The deed that follows upon thinking institutionally is action that follows from the purpose for having the whole apparatus of a school system in the first place. That purpose—the morality of aspiration institutionally expressed—is the education of the next generation.

This is what I meant above when I recommended focusing on the background so that we can see, through the expectations about rightful behavior, "enactments of trust in identity amid assumptions of institutional purpose." This has been called "system trust." People are who they appear to be, doing what they are supposed to do, with things proceeding in basically proper order. It makes communication and a healthy social life possible.[1]

Practice will inevitably fall short. Other agendas will intervene. But in the relationship between teacher and student, the one with the assumed authority of a teacher to teach and the other with the need and opportunity of a student to learn, this is the basic institutional aspiration by which we know we are falling short and being distracted by other agendas.

What then is it to act institutionally? The specific deeds will vary depending on the particular institutional order. Earlier we noted that the person who rushes to save the family photo album rather than the television from a house fire is acting in an appropriate manner with regard to the family as an institution. The same person fleeing a fire in his office building has failed to act in an institutionally appropriate way if he grabs the family photos on his desk rather than the discs containing the firm's vital business records. So we cannot pretend to compile a list of institutionally right and wrong deeds. As in the earlier discussion of thinking institutionally, the discussion has to proceed by using concepts at a more general, midlevel range. And here, unfortunately, we have only tattered modern remnants of the concepts that could shed light on this matter of acting institutionally. The three main concepts are profession, office, and stewardship. In discussing these three concepts, we are elaborating on what at the onset of this book I simply called "respect-in-depth." Each of the three following concepts points to a way of honoring something by one's own appropriate participation in its practice.

Profession

Today's idea of a profession is impoverished because our modern way of thinking about professions is intensely anti-institutional. By now it should be clear that by "anti-institutional" I do not mean that modern professions are opposed to organizations or bureaucratic forms. Modern professional education is entirely embedded in bureaucratic organizations. In the schools and systems of internships one learns the cognitive content of the profession and all the technical skills relevant to applying that content. No, our modern way of thinking about professions is strongly anti-institutional because it leaves as an afterthought the whole orientation of the profession to moral purposes.[2] Seen from the inside, the profession amounts to a particular technical expertise that produces personal career success. Seen from the outside, any profession appears as a collection of individuals monopolizing a body of technical knowledge and the practice of those specialized techniques. Often the notion of rational self-interest is added to make the point that members of a profession are in a position to use their monopoly to extract rent. Of course, if this is what a profession means, it lacks anything resembling the institutional appreciation I am trying to bring into view.

The institutional view of a profession reflects premodern ideas having to do with a certain kind of noble "calling." In this view the professional embodies a deeply held sense of responding to the call of worthwhile purposes beyond oneself. That call and response are identity forming. Being a member of a profession means more than acquiring a body of theory and set of techniques, though it does mean that. It also means a principled way of being in the world. To invoke claims of professionalism is to appeal to standards for guiding and judging conduct that go beyond technical knowledge or personal career success. One enters into a professional community whose common technical skills are understood in light of ethical standards and fiduciary responsibilities that are endorsed, monitored, and enforced by one's peers. Even in a profession as technically demanding as engineering, trust is evoked not so much through assertions of expertise as through a reliable social process by which professional knowledge is produced and applied.[3]

Thus professionals aspire to a shared normative vision of what it is to be in a given profession. Are we talking about something real here? An answer to that question can be found by recalling your own encounters with individual doctors, nurses, teachers, or lawyers. It is when you deal with someone who does not perform in a "professional" manner that you learn to appreciate those who do.

Before the cultural upheaval known as the 1960s, the modern model of technical professionalism appeared secure. The "competence gap" in the professional–client relationship seemed to ensure deference to professional authority. And while the relationship was normally characterized by dominance and dependence, there was also an expectation of trust based on shared values, such as health or education, and the translation of those values into shared professional–client goals, such as curing the patient or teaching the student.[4] Since the 1960s, the professional-client relationship has been one more aspect of life caught up in the swirling distrust of institutions that we observed at the beginning of this book.

The doctor-patient encounter is a good example. Most people would probably agree it is a good thing that the model of dominance and dependence in this relationship has been giving way to persuasion and shared information.[5] However, that is obviously not the full story. Under pressure from patient activist groups and economic advocates of managed care, the doctor has been receding as a professional figure to become a health care "provider." This provider is now dealing with a health care "consumer" shopping for medical services, as well as a potentially wronged party now protected by new laws and courts.[6] In the new world of patient advocacy, online doctor ratings, consumer protection, entitlements, and litigation, high-minded talk about autonomous professional responsibility seems quaint at best. It is a world that equates trust in professionalism with gullibility. In this contemporary context, the doctor becomes less of a professional in a normative professional community and more of a service supplier and potential litigant engaged in defensive actions.

In recent years the problem of an ethical vacuum in professional education—where academic bureaucracies are under immense financial pressures to descend into mere professional training—has been recognized by various institutional leaders. Some professional schools have created full-fledged ethics programs, and it seems that most such schools now have at least a required course in professional ethics or courses in which the theme of ethical standards is emphasized.[7] Obviously, this is all to the good if one cares about acting institutionally in the professions. However, they are only courses, and they may amount to nothing more than the required attendance at chapel that was once a feature of almost all U.S. colleges, to dubious effect. What is clear is that the cultural, economic, and political forces pushing in the opposite direction are immense and relentless.

Office

Another threadbare concept potentially relevant to acting institutionally is the idea of "office." In fact this notion may be so
threadbare by now that, like the poor man's sock accumulating
ever more holes, it has simply disappeared. The analogy fails,
however, because the concept has disappeared not from use but
from neglect and misuse. Perhaps the most that can be said for
our modern view of "the office" is that, by virtue of a television
series, it is a running joke on the setting in which people exhibit
an amusing repertoire of dysfunctional behavior.

Still, since I began by claiming that this book is an effort at
recovery and articulation on behalf of things unfashionable, we
cannot let a television show have the last word. So for purposes
of action in an institutionally relevant way, we should consider
the concept of office and the claims it makes on behavior.

The concepts of profession and office both carry connota-
tions of morally obligated action, but they are not the same
thing. A profession entails a particular body of knowledge and
techniques being "professed"—on offer—to clients. In this
sense, the concept of office is less weighted with substantive
content. But that does not mean it is a morally lesser concept.
"Office," in its rich, premodern sense, has to do with obligations to act by virtue of being "positioned" in a certain place.
Because of that positional quality, the term "office" lent itself in
modern times to being shrunk down into meaning nothing
more than the buildings or rooms serving as a "place" of business. Yet this is indeed a tattered remnant of the concept that we
need to draw upon. The richer concept is about occupying, not
a physical place, but a moral space in society. Recalling the distinction made at the end of Chapter 3, the emphasis here is on
the morality of duty rather than aspiration.

The term "office" comes down to us from the Latin,
mainly by way of the Roman classics and church history. Com-
pounded from the words for "work" and "to do," *officium* indicates the performance of a task, with heavy overtones of a duty

to perform properly. Thus Cicero's great book *De Officiis* is translated *On Duties*. It was from Cicero's *De Officiis* that David Hume would take his *Catalogue of Virtues* and Dante his classification of sins in the *Inferno*.

With the rise of Christianity and the organized church, *officium* took on added meaning. It meant being charged with special duty and trust of a more sacred nature, as in Paul, "an apostle of the gentiles," magnifying his "office" (Romans 11:13).

Church reformers such as Gregory VII and Bernard of Clairvaux sought to clean up widespread disorder and abuses among the clergy by purifying the vision of the priest's office and its duties of selfless service. Office also became a way of conceptualizing the particular duties of place within the church. Thus Aquinas distinguished between the *officium praelationis* (the administrative office) of bishops and the *officium magisterii* (the teaching office) of theologians as a way of emphasizing that the theologian is a genuine teacher and not simply a spokesman for higher officers in the medieval church. "Office" also spoke to ceremonial duty and service, as in the daily eight hourly prayers of the church or offices of Mass and the last rites in the "office of the dead."

With even this brief background, we can sense how in the later Middle Ages the concept of office could migrate from the ecclesiastical realm of church structure to the increasingly powerful realm of secular political structures expressing allegiance to princes and kings. "Office" could be a special duty and trust conferred on positions under constituted civil authority, as in a treasury office or judicial office. And the concept could be broadened out still further into an increasingly vibrant postmedieval society. "Office" could mean a customary duty that arises from the relations between people, as in the case of Shakespeare's Page, who says: "Sir, he is within; and I would I could do a good office between you" *(The Merry Wives of Windsor)*. "Office" also could and did come to mean "function"—but not in our modern, antiseptic social science way. It is function that answers to duty in light of what a particular thing is designed and meant to do, as in Shakespeare's powerful characterization of the human eye: "her eyes are fled/into the deep dark cabins of her head:/Where they resign their office and their light/to the disposing of her troubled brain" (*Venus and Adonis*).

What can we learn from this little background study of the term "office"? We can learn to appreciate an enriched sense—an "office-oriented" understanding—of performance in the daily tasks of life. It is not necessary to settle for the mentality and teachings of people who are adept at making popular television programs. If we are willing to disenthrall ourselves and seek something more authentic, there is available a historically rich concept of office that speaks to that part of us that does not want to spend the day just going through the motions. That voice of duty and service obligates a person by virtue of his or her position in a larger, worthwhile scheme of things.[8] One need not be part of some learned profession in order to act institutionally. And one need not be in some high public position in order to hold and fulfill an office.

This may all seem very abstract and theoretical, but the fact of the matter is that there are few things more realistic and "practical" than the idea of office in a person's head. Consider another situation that most people reading this sentence have certainly shared: entrusting your car to a mechanic for the day. If you could know it, what is the most practical, realistically important thing you would want to know? It is not the mechanic's credentials, since he may be skilled but dishonest. It is not how long he has been a mechanic, since it may have been time spent ripping off customers. It is certainly not his income, age, race, friendships, or ethnic background. What we would most like to know is this person's commitment to doing the best job he can as a mechanic, not just on his family's and friends' cars but anybody's car. Given that such an inner mental picture is inaccessible to us, we use proxies for it, such as the mechanic's reputation around town or the track record of the garage that employs him. In any event, we should not doubt that a person's view of duty to the expectations of a position, the office, is a very practical matter.

For most of us, being in the world of work is not a question of having what would be regarded as a "profession," at least not as discussed in the preceding section. What most people have are jobs. And as the economy has reflected the growing impact of an integrating world economy, what people especially have is a succession of jobs. In fact, résumé-building through a succession of jobs has become a modern art form. As before, we should try to peer behind the foreground features of what our résumés look like and consider what lies in the background. The central feature of the modern résumé is that it is entirely self-centered, an account of personal qualifications defined through past jobs. The dictionary definition of the term "job" captures this modern viewpoint. A "job" is (1) a miscellaneous piece of work undertaken on order at a stated rate, (2) something done for private advantage, and (3) a task that has to be done. A job is a view of human activity that implies no larger meaning beyond the tasked Self.

Of course, it is possible to spell out the "duties" associated with a job. But doing that really amounts only to a listing of the specific tasks to be performed. It is the job description. A concept of office subordinates the Self to larger normative responsibilities, and that makes it more difficult to stipulate an "office description." This is because an office carries with it obligations of a general nature that reach beyond any laundry list of tasks to be performed. A job is discharged by performing according to assigned, mechanistic specifications. An office is discharged by understanding and carrying out the proper purpose and spirit of the work. There is therefore a fiduciary quality in office-holding that is missing from job-doing. In a sense, one is trusted to understand and do what is expected of a competent person in such a position.

While it is useful to distinguish between having a job and holding an office, it is more important to recognize that it is possible to have an "office-oriented" understanding of a job. This means acting out of an underlying loyalty to the purpose or purposes that lie behind there being such a job in the first place. In everyday life we constantly encounter the difference between jobbers and officeholders. The salesclerk who attends to the customer, volunteers to help, and actually seems intent on providing a service stands out in memory from other "service personnel" who are merely doing a job. The auto mechanic who is a jobber will perform the minimal checklist of tasks found in the manual. The authentic mechanic will not be so mechanical. The checklist of tasks will be done within a larger concern for doing what it takes to get the car in good working order. Not to know or care about general expectations beyond the task at hand simplifies the workday, but it also drains away any chance for meaning and fulfillment while you are "putting in your time."

Usually we think about offices in relation to public institutions. And there it is painfully obvious that being in an office, such as the presidency, does not ensure that a person will act "presidentially." The same applies to legislative office. Given the strenuous process required to "win" such positions, there is a powerful temptation to treat them as prizes rather than offices. The prize may carry benefits and burdens, but what gets lost from sight amid the intense maneuvering and rush of events is the idea itself of being a legislator. There is good evidence that the U.S. Congress is suffering as an institution because it is full of people who do not seem to understand themselves primarily in terms of being legislators.[9] Likewise by virtue of their office, judges are under a duty to apply legal rules that may produce outcomes at odds with their personal preferences. This has not prevented leading judicial figures from acting more like legislators when, despite being unelected, they have felt it necessary to legislate complex social changes in the name of progress.[10]

However, public offices are not our focus issue here. Our aim has been to see the duties of position more broadly. A person with a sense of office acts institutionally in any sphere of life. As Cicero put it, "For no part of life, neither public affairs nor private, neither in the forum nor at home, neither when acting on our own nor in dealings with another, can be free from duty. Everything that is honourable in a life depends upon its cultivation, and everything dishonourable upon its neglect."[11]

Thus we arrive at an utterly unfashionable view of office that can encompass even family relationships. Fashion aside, given the widespread sense of disorder in modern family life, it is a view worth considering on its merits and not for its alignment with conventional opinion of the day. For example, offices in the family pertain to the duties of parents and children. Arguably, a parent who does no more than teach a child to think for himself—for fear of imposing morals or being judgmental—has abdicated the office of parent.[12] The duty of that office is to serve the well-being of the child. Such well-being is not likely to be served by letting a child think he can be a law unto himself, as if the child's office is somehow to live independent of guidance and supervision. That does not mean swinging to the other extreme of trying to control every aspect of a child's life by simply handing down rules and sanctions. Between the two extremes are rules of right conduct that will help a child attain a usable freedom that is worth having. With adulthood comes the former child's responsibility to think for himself about the moral standards taught and modeled by his parents. It is significant that Cicero addresses his book *On Duties* to his twenty-one-year-old son Marcus with the admonition that "you must use your own judgment about the content."

The term "role" has largely supplanted "office" as a way of characterizing behavior in light of expectations. We have the anthropologists and sociologists to thank for that. And to be sure, role analysis has proven to be a very fruitful concept in a great deal of academic work over the past seventy-five years.[13] But when people live their lives in terms of a social science category, something is backward and wrong. Widespread and careless use of the notion of "role" indicates an impoverished modern view of human activity. That is because in substituting role for office there is a significant change in moral perspective. It is the difference between acting a part and fulfilling the responsibilities of a position. Individuals who see their lives as an assembly of roles may find many ways of expressing themselves. But they may never realize that there is an office called adulthood with expected ways for grownups to act.

Within its particular confines, an office-oriented view is respectful of the whole person because it entails the obligation actually to *be* something. Human personhood resists decomposition into a collection of play-acting roles or job specifications. Action as an officeholder is not only a way of acting institutionally. It is also a way of being something in the world. In this sense, "office" differs from "job" or "role" as "person" differs from "individual." Within its own limits, the former sees an integrated, socially connected whole, while the latter sees only an isolated point on the space-time grid.

Stewardship

We might say that if "profession" is about content and "office" is about position, stewardship is about process. That formula is, of course, too neat and should not be pushed to extremes. In its origins, the notion of stewardship was clearly attached to a well-defined and honored position (a person entrusted with managing a master's household) as well as a substantive competence (the art of *oikonoma* [economy], or prudent management of a household's affairs). Nonetheless, the formula has some value because it is the processive quality of stewardship that I would like to emphasize in taking this final look at what it means to act institutionally.

As a process, stewardship has a beginning, middle, and end. This narrative quality arises from the essential idea of acting on behalf of an absent owner. In the ancient world of Greece and Rome, with landed estates and the masters of those households frequently away on matters of public and private business, there was a very concrete social quality to the notion of stewardship. Likewise, in a remote province of the Roman Empire, Jesus could speak parables about good and bad stewards to his mostly Jewish listeners and know that people in that part of the Mediterranean world could understand what he was talking about (Luke 12:42; 16:1). The centuries came and went, empires and barbarians with them, but the concept remained relevant for pointing toward human actions intended to express a certain kind of relationship. The Greek and Roman sources were largely lost to memory, but one could still hear the concept echoing in the Old English of a medieval world. The physical expression of the lord's great household, his "hall," was his *sti,* and the person or persons looking after its well-being were the keepers or wardens, his *weard.* In more modern times the social concreteness of "sti-weard"-ship has been buried under layers of abstraction, such that today only legal professionals can understand and apply the technical terminology of "trusts, trusteeships, powers of attorney," and the like. However, if we seek to understand what it means to act institutionally, we cannot leave the subject confined to legal casebooks. Stewardship needs to be retrieved and articulated as an aspect of practical human activity.[14]

Stewardship begins with the act of entrusting. For the steward, this means being put in charge of something that belongs to someone else. That term, "entrusted," is important because it emphasizes that the point of departure for stewardship is not just any kind of trusting relationship. This is trust of a very high, fiduciary quality.[15] It is not a trust derived from calculating the expected probability of the steward's doing this or that particular thing. With stewardship there is an end in view—the owner's return and an accounting for management of his property—but there is no constant monitoring or attempt at detailed control of performance. Stewardship means leaving your affairs in another's hands with the belief that this person will do right by you.[16] The opportunity for abuse is therefore immense. From the steward's side this phase is what the preceding chapter called "faithful reception."

Living in our modern society we have little choice about entering into stewardship relationships. As a practical matter we are forced every day to entrust our household affairs to stewards. They are the managing overseers of our "property." That sounds an odd statement if we are thinking of property as so much physical stuff—land, houses, cars, furniture, and the like. Surely, aren't we managing our stuff ourselves?

Here the legal understandings can give us a better insight. Physical objects are simply physical objects. Your property resides in your right to use those objects. The substantive value of property lies in the right to use it, and if that right is destroyed the physical object may remain but your property in the object is annihilated. Thus the Bill of Rights is not really about printing presses, assembly halls, churches, firearms, and the like. It is about protecting citizens' property as the right to use such things freely. And so Madison could write after winning passage of the Bill of Rights: "[A] man has a property in his opinions, and the free communication of them. He has a property of peculiar value in his religious opinions and in the profession and practice dictated by them. He has a property very dear to him in the safety and liberty of his person. He has an equal property in the free use of his faculties, and free choice of the objects on which to employ them. In a word, as a man is said to have a right to his property, he may equally be said to have a property in his rights."[17]

Regarding our property in this sense, contemporary life gives us very little choice but to enter into stewardshiplike relationships every day. The modern corporation, with its legal and moral responsibility for managing the property of owners, is an obvious example. However, this necessity for entrusting extends well beyond the matter of being a stockholder in any corporation. Our property in a house or apartment is entrusted to a vast apparatus of rules, regulations, and enforcement mechanisms. We are comfortable entering into a contract with a stranger because we have entrusted our property in contracting to that apparatus, which we believe will intervene if necessary to enforce the contract's terms. The property in what Madison called our opinions, faculties, safety, and liberty of our person is entrusted to the protection of the very governmental apparatus that can do so much to threaten those rights. That is why over the decades the claim has been repeatedly made that administration in public and private organizations should be conceived as a process of stewardship.[18]

Following the act of entrusting, the second phase of stewardship is faithful management. This is the heart of the matter. To modern ears, the term "stewardship" can sound rather passive, simply a kind of house-sitting until the owner returns. In fact it is more like house-sitting on steroids. The long-standing expectation has been that stewardship entails very active management. Even the notion of guardianship is inadequate if it is taken to mean only defensive action.

Historically, the steward's tasks included supervision of servants, collection of rents, investing in new initiatives, and keeping of accounts. Unlike today, what constituted "good" management was not something that needed to be negotiated or pondered over by academics. Good was defined by the purpose for which the stewardship relationship was put into effect. Affairs were to be managed for the owner's welfare just as if the owner were managing those affairs himself. Anything short of that was not good management. Thus it may sound harsh to us, but the audience hearing Jesus's parable of the nobleman and the ten servants would have immediately understood the rationale behind the message (Luke 19:12). The servant who merely hid what he had been entrusted with, in order to return it intact to the owner, deserved no reward. What he deserved and received was condemnation.

This example serves to emphasize that stewardship entails a heavier responsibility than the concept of usufruct we discussed in the last chapter. Stewardship means acting in a much more "institutional" way. We might recall that Jefferson used the idea of usufruct to underscore the entitlement of each generation to enjoy fully the product of its unowned assets. It was a present existence without strings, except that the assets themselves must be passed on intact. It was the mentality of a tenant insisting on the full enjoyment of the rights of the living generation. By contrast, Madison's response illuminated something more closely resembling a stewardship mentality—acknowledging indebtedness to those from whom one has received, and likewise the obligation to invest on behalf of the owner(s) to whom the assets will be passed on in the future. So it is that actions based on stewardship might be characterized as a kind of truncated Golden Rule—to serve another as that person would serve himself. This reemphasizes the basic point: stewardship is calling on a very high standard of fiduciary responsibility.

What can we say in our own times about acting from a sense of stewardship? Probably the most that can be said is that there are wisps of such a thing floating around, landing here and there to produce nostalgic exhortations (which is, of course, the same thing that can be said about the book you are reading). For example, the case of *Meinhard v. Salmon* is still taught in some of the nation's best business schools. It provides a splendid exhortation.

A real estate partnership was formed between one Morton Meinhard as investor and Walter Salmon, his coinvestor and active manager of the partnership. They renovated a building in Manhattan and as partners entered into a twenty-year lease on the building, making an excellent return. Four months before the twenty-year lease expired, and with his partner Meinhard left in the dark, manager Salmon signed an eighty-year lease agreement with a new owner envisioning a vastly more profitable renovation of the property. Meinhard naturally asked Salmon to make the new lease an asset to be shared in the twenty-year partnership which was about to end. Salmon refused to recognize any such obligation and claimed the added proceeds for himself. In ringing language, the chief justice of the New York Supreme Court, Benjamin Cardoza, affirmed the fiduciary responsibilities of a manager's stewardship: "Joint adventurers, like co-partners, owe to one another, while the enterprise continues, the duty of the finest loyalty. Many forms of conduct permissible in a workaday world for those acting at arm's length are forbidden to those bound by fiduciary ties. A trustee is held to something stricter than the morals of the market place. Not honesty alone, but the punctilio of an honor the most sensitive, is then the standard of behavior."[19]

This is a fine exhortatory example of the claims I referred to earlier—the commendation of stewardship as a guiding standard in public and private management. But the case *Meinhard v. Salmon* was decided in 1928. While it is taught today in some business school courses on ethics, its message of stewardship seems an anachronism that is easily overwhelmed by the way contemporary organizations work. The teachers in our leading business schools dare not say it, but *Meinhard v. Salmon* is mainly a testimony to the world we have lost. Economic incentives within today's investment industry consistently and rather thoroughly smother calls to fiduciary responsibility.[20]

Whether public or private, "management" is not really a profession in contemporary society. There are no standards of ethical behavior endorsed and enforced by the peers in one's so-called profession.[21] Likewise, whether public or private, the modern concept of office is confined to notions of bureaucratic structure largely devoid of moral commitments. And if we try to call into play the long-revered notion of stewardship, the plain fact is that managers in our society exhibit few signs of such self-awareness. Nor do they have much reason to do so, given the vast incentive structure rewarding other kinds of short-term performance. In summarizing various surveys that have examined how public and private managers view the responsibilities of their work, two researchers conclude: "The evidence suggests that public and private administrators as a class appear to care little about their obligations to be trustworthy stewards."[22]

To repeat what I said at the outset of this section, as we consider what it means to act institutionally we are living with the tattered remnants of premodern concepts trying to express what I have called respect-in-depth. They call on a person's actions to be characterized by an ongoing commitment to the value and integrity of some institutional enterprise. In this case, the conceptual remnant is the notion of stewardship in its active, management phase.

The third phase of the stewardship process is the return of the owner's property. With this comes an accounting to show that the property with which the steward has been entrusted is in "good" order. And we can now understand that this means a positive performance and not a mere passive, dig-a-hole-for-safekeeping approach.

Of course, the problem here is that in modern times we will not see the owner coming over the hill with his caravan to resume management of his property. If there is to be an accounting for stewardship, it cannot be done by the simple face-to-face relationships of the past. Neither can the accounting be treated as a onetime event, since, as noted earlier, the stewardship relation for protecting our property is a pervasive, inescapable, and never-ending condition in modern society. So it is that beginning with the industrialization and urbanization of the nineteenth century, we have created a vast array of mechanisms to reassure people that their affairs are being properly managed.[23] This accountability machinery is largely taken for granted and occupies a major part of what passes for the routines of daily life in contemporary society. It includes rules for record-keeping, reporting requirements, audits, lawsuits, regulatory agencies, Freedom of Information and election laws, oversight committees, investigative reporting, watchdog groups, and a host of other rules that we lump together with the name "red tape."

No one would deny the importance of accountability. It is an integral part of the stewardship process. But what we witness over time in modern society is an increasingly layered system of guardians monitoring guardians. As this process continues there are few moments of thoroughgoing accountability and thousands of tiny instances for giving a procedural account of this and that action. But adding up micro-accountabilities does not produce macro-accountability. It is in fact more likely than not to obscure it. It is like judging a pitcher's performance by summing up assessments of each one of his pitches. That never tells you the important big thing, which is whether he won the game.

If accountability is our only approach to creating and sustaining stewardship, then we are lost in an infinite regress, of setting stewards to watch stewards to watch stewards. In this section I have argued that one way of acting institutionally is to self-consciously choose to behave in the ways of stewardship. This means receiving in trust, faithfully managing on behalf of the absent owner, and standing ready to give an account.

What we tend to forget within our layered systems of supposed accountability is that stewards first have to aspire to stewardship. The desire to serve has to be willingly taken up and be there in the steward's heart and mind. Its presence can be confirmed or disconfirmed by accountability procedures, but it can never be "accountable-ized" into existence.

However, stewardship can be "accountable-ized" out of existence, and that is probably the condition we have reached today.[24] Our society is clogged with multiple accountability processes to the point of dissolving stewardship and its sense of responsibility into nonexistence. This is done in a vain effort to control the discretionary actions of people whom we put into positions of trust, and then do everything possible to show that we do not consider them trustworthy.

Dangers

So far I have spent a great deal of time emphasizing the positive aspects of thinking institutionally. Obviously there is another side, and that is what we want to consider here.

Slavery was something supported by a good deal of institutional thinking. It was an institution sustained by people taking "faithful reception" of established ways. It was infused with values of racial superiority and intergenerational rationales of mutual obligation for "the Southern way of life." Likewise, the Mafia would appear to be an outstanding example of institutional thinking and loyalty across the generations. Or consider an even harder case. To judge from his speeches and writings, Adolph Hitler apparently epitomized all the requirements for thinking and acting institutionally. He saw himself taking faithful reception of the ancient myths of Aryan racial purity and German nationhood. Everything he did seemed infused with value and purpose beyond the requirements of the immediate task at hand (much to the distaste of the German army's professional leadership). He stretched time horizons not only to the next few generations but to a thousand-year millennial future. And as for stewardship, suffice it to say that Hitler saw himself merging his very being with the larger historical phenomenon of the German nation.

But we need not go to such extremes in order to throw doubt on any wholehearted endorsement of thinking and acting institutionally. Those average citizens upholding institutions of sexism, paternalism, class privilege, and religious intolerance have brought misery to untold millions of human beings. And even with the most genteel, elitist touch, anti-Semitism remains anti-Semitism. It was with the idea of protecting their institution that Harvard officials in the 1920s created admission rules allowing for discretionary review of merit. In the name of that higher cause, the aim was to limit Jewish enrollment and ensure a sufficient number of White Anglo-Saxon-Protestant "paying guests."[25]

These examples insist on a question, but they do not answer it. Is thinking and acting institutionally necessarily doing so on behalf of a "good" cause?

I think it is important to acknowledge that in writing a book on institutions, this is the sort of deeply searching question that should give a person pause. It is a question that deserves careful reflection, not a quick and easy answer so that the author can march on to the next phase of a book's argument. What we really have to come to grips with is the notion of "good" and "bad" institutions. Just as conservatism is only as good as what it conserves, institutional thinking is only as good or bad as what it is institutionalizing.

There will be some of a positivist persuasion in the social sciences who regard this as a "scientifically" inappropriate distinction. In that view, social scientists' professional role is to study institutions and institutional behavior and so far as possible leave aside personal opinions of moral worth (which they may appropriately advocate as citizens in the political arena). This is a plausible position within the strict confines of rational technique. The social scientist's aim is to acquire a more accurate understanding of the social world. Gathering and analyzing data to fit one's moral preconceptions and preferences are not rational means to that end.

However, a larger indifference to the matter of goodness or badness—that is, the moral quality—of institutions makes no rational sense either in terms of social science or human goals. Being rational, human beings (and this includes social scientists) pursue a more accurate understanding of the social world for a purpose, not for its own sake. That purpose is, in one way or another, to enhance human well-being. Any social science committed to a fine impartiality between the institutional causes of an Adolph Hitler or a Mother Theresa amounts to a human absurdity. The best that can be said about it is that this position—a social science in pursuit of understanding without moral purpose—makes sense only if such investigations are to be regarded as objects of aesthetic appreciation for their own sake. The cure for that view is to read the articles and books published by social scientists. Aesthetic value is not the first thing that comes to mind.

One way to try to dodge the problem of judging institutions—and thus institutional thinking within its respective context—as "good" or "bad" is to treat such judgments as simply another variety of observable, descriptive data. Just as people have different political party allegiances or economic preferences, they have different value judgments about different institutions. As an allegedly detached observer, a social scientist can describe, analyze, and perhaps even go some way toward explaining these positions without personally making any claims about the moral worth of different institutions. For example, in a theory developed by the late anthropologist Mary Douglas, there are four basic types of "cultural institutions" with distinctive values and social relations that, in a sense, play against each other. These broad categories are hierarchy, egalitarianism, individualism, and fatalism (or isolation). People whose values legitimize egalitarian social relations think hierarchical institutions are bad; hierarchs think egalitarian institutions are bad, and so on.[26] It is all in the eye of the beholder.

This is obviously a dodge, because it only delays the inevitable necessity for moral choice. It is true that a great deal of time can be spent gathering and analyzing the research data concerning people's moral preferences about what is being institutionalized or deinstitutionalized. But at the end of the day there has to be some purpose and human use to this analytic activity. If it is all just knowledge for knowledge's sake, we are back to some sort of dubious aesthetic justification or pointless assertion that "curious minds want to know."

Social scientists search for accurate, reliable knowledge about the social world because they are supposed to want to know the truth of things. And that desire to know what is true about man's social existence has a purpose. This purpose is not an arbitrary whim or intellectual postulate. It is embedded in human nature. Of all the creatures that might be studied, it is in the unique nature of human beings not to be satisfied that they simply exist. That they want more than brute existence is proven by evidence lying all around us in the form of various human civilizations. Among the things they want by virtue of being human is somehow to enhance their well-being. That is not a view imposed on the evidence. It is what the evidence says. It says it wherever we find humans existing, however static or dynamic, ancient or modern the society. We are creatures who consciously struggle with questions of not only who we are but also what we ought to do for our own good.

Modern social science did not appear on this scene in the past hundred-plus years as if dropped from the heavens. In the name of gaining accurate knowledge about human affairs, the "institution" of social science took up its task in light of the purpose that makes human activity human—to learn more about how to advance human well-being. However austere and scientifically impersonal their work might appear, that vaguely defined purpose lies at the beginning and end of social scientists' institutional enterprise. In that, social scientists cannot help themselves. They're only being human.

The same perspective applies for evaluating the moral worth of institutions. Morally speaking, to think and act institutionally may be positive or negative depending on what ends are being served. But those ends are not arbitrary. They are not whatever institutional authorities might say. Institutions exist for people. People do not exist for institutions. Since institutions exist for people, they are to be judged along a moral continuum of good and bad according to what is needed for human beings to flourish as human beings. In order to deserve the designation of good, institutions ought to be doing what is good for us as human beings.

What, then, is good for us as human beings, that institutions might be judged in serving such purposes? Just because there are libraries of books devoted to answering that question does not justify pretending that we do not know the general outlines of an answer. It comes through reason and experience tested against the judgment of centuries of religious thought and philosophical inquiry. This wisdom is not obscure or inaccessible to the common man. Human beings flourish in seeking conditions of justice, freedom, equality, and community with each other. Obviously, these and other goods of human life are often in conflict with each other, a fact that lends both a tragic and heroic quality to all our strivings. Our disagreements on how these conditions for human well-being are to be realized are vast and complex. But that is not saying we are without rudder and polestar, with all the deckhands scrambling over purely subjective impositions of personal values. We can argue about injustice, oppression, inequality, and alienation among people because we know that they are the negation of what is good for us as human beings.

Despite all their particularities, institutions are embedded in a larger moral order of beneficence toward human well-being. They are to heal not injure, educate not stifle, nourish not kill, t seek fairness not injustice, practice honesty not fraud, and so on.

For this reason, among all the institutions that might be observed, special care must always be given to the two "superintending" institutions of the modern era: law and government. Today they are probably our most popular targets for ridicule and jokes. However, they are also the two institutions that we depend on to oversee the tensioned relationships among all the other institutions. The "good" or "bad" performance of legal and governmental institutions shapes the environment for sustaining or undermining the performance of all the other institutional orders in society. Despite all the jokes, most people are likely to understand this. They recognize that it is one thing for a player to cheat but quite another thing to discover that the referees in a sport have been cheating. The former tarnishes a game; the latter strikes at its heart.

Here then is the danger. Whenever we are tempted to speak of the "intrinsic worth" of an institution—such as might require subordination of some people to other people, claims of general welfare over individual freedom, or the call to personal sacrifice—there is a warning bell that should go off if institutions are to be judged by their true purpose. Since people are not created for the good of institutions but institutions for the purposes of people, any call to the intrinsic worth of an institution is a lie if it does not ultimately recognize and serve the moral and ontological primacy of human persons and their well-being.[27] To repeat, that means institutions exist for people and for serving their good. People do not exist for institutions. When institutions are doing ill, it is as a parasitic version of what institutions are supposed to be as agents for human good. From the standpoint of that moral norm you can recognize its absence in "bad" institutions and see what needs remedy in other institutions' performance. But the reverse does not apply. A sighted person can understand darkness, but you cannot explain light and color to a person who has always been blind. From the moral emptiness of bad institutions you cannot understand what a good institution might be.

In this light we can return to the hard cases of slavery and Nazism. Repulsed as we are by their efforts, a great many Southern slaveholders as well as nonslaveholders did seek to offer "good" institutional reasons for defending their way of life. Hypocrisy and self-serving rationalizations were certainly a large part of this effort at justification. But they were not the whole story. To insist that they were is to prefer preening in our own self-righteousness rather than seeking serious historical understanding. The Southern ideology upheld a corporate social ethic that was based on a legacy of orthodox Christian theology, learned classical studies, and literal biblical exegesis. It was a morally grounded outlook that could unite Southern slaveholders and nonslaveholders alike in the conviction that the institution of slavery, when rightly managed, was ordained by God. God's chosen people, the Jews, had been a slaveholding people and suffered no divine reprimand for being so. In this view, the ugly facts of slavery had to be reformed so as to meet the required Christian character of a slave society. The master–slave relationship was under a moral obligation to live up to the standards of the Abramic household and the teachings of the Gospels.[28]

Granted, to modern readers all this can sound preposterous, to put it politely. Only if we are willing to enter into their admittedly foreign framework of institutional thinking can we hear what at least some well-intentioned Southerners concerned for human welfare were trying to say. In looking ahead, they could contrast a modern slaveholding republic with the emerging European example of deadly class warfare between capital and "free labor." What they thought they could see was a possible future of rural independence, domestic servitude based on humane personal relationships, and general social tranquility. And they saw this standing in stark contrast to class hostilities that would be produced by the forced mobilization of socially isolated "free" laborers dominated by centralized structures of industrial capital and governmental power. Misguided as it was, we should recognize that it was an effort at moral reasoning about the ultimate human purpose of institutions. By opening our ears to hear that, we can also gain a greater appreciation for Lincoln's superior moral reasoning about the "mystic chords of memory" linking the Declaration of Independence, the Constitution, and a people in sacred union.

The "Hitler problem" as regards thinking institutionally is something quite different. It is the sort of problem that only someone yearning to look clever would even dare to raise. Everything about the man Adolph Hitler was a monstrous perversion of institutional thinking. If his example somehow resembles it, that is only because Nazism was in every respect a parasitic distortion of the real thing. Hitler and his Nazi movement "faithfully took delivery" of only the diseased, anti-Semitic elements of the German past. He and his fellow thugs willfully dismissed the larger legacies of Goethe, Bach, Luther, and everything else humane and elevating to the human spirit. The values Hitler sought to infuse were a sweet and tasty brew of lies about racial superiority and German history. The truth of things was irrelevant. In its place was a pseudoscience devoted to Aryanism and a phony history about German national identity. As for Hitler's delusional view of a future "1,000-year Reich," his obligation to the future amounted to a Reich lasting barely ten years and bequeathing only mass destruction to the next generation. In the end, Hitler's "stewardship" was of the type that—facing the personal failure in 1945 he so richly deserved—then determined to destroy the German nation that had proven itself unworthy of him. Any person of common sense will recognize that this was a monomaniac, not a steward.

★ ★ ★

So far we have considered the danger of forgetting the moral purpose of institutions. There are also some very practical dangers to anyone who takes seriously what I have been trying to say in this book. Some of the costs of thinking institutionally are greater than others, but in any event they need to be weighed and counted.

First, thinking institutionally is likely to endanger your standing as a sophisticated thinker. Granted, word of this terrible fate will be confined mainly to academic and related intellectual circles, but these are the circles in which people use ideas to try to make sense of the world. They are the places from which intellectuals tell the rest of society how to think about its problems. In this setting today the critic of all things institutional appears shrewd and liberated. The task is to see through things. Institutions are tools for manipulation, and their values are disguises for self-interest. Rational arguments on behalf of an institutional order are rationalizations for the exercise of power. Suspicion and mistrust are the signs of a sharp mind.

By comparison a person caught thinking institutionally will appear naive and gullible. It means that, perhaps at your best, you are a lapsed "critical thinker." You argue that if many people did not believe in institutional values and purposes it would make no sense to hide behind and try to manipulate them. If rational arguments for an institutional order are simply a fraud, there would be no grounds for the rationalizations by which people could let themselves be defrauded. Ah, but there, your critic will say, you show your weakness as a sophisticated thinker. You are too much like those ordinary people who cannot see through things. Real intellectuals can do that. You, poor fellow, risk being a mere moralist.

Second, anyone committed to thinking and acting institutionally can expect to remain obscure and unappreciated. There is no celebrity status to be achieved in this line of work, and in our contemporary society a great many people will regard that as a major cost. There may be moments of crisis, but for the most part the care and nurturing of institutional values is a behind-the-scenes activity that no one in any of the media, old or new, will consider newsworthy. If all goes well there might be an eventual certificate of appreciation for "conscientious performance of duty."[29] But it is not something one should expect.

Third, when your work is noticed you can expect it to be routinely misunderstood. The writer Edward Abbey noted that in a corrupt society, the sneakiest form of subtlety is to speak the plain truth. To those interested only in "bottom-line results," your commitment to institutional values will be seen as unresponsive and obstructionist. You can expect to be regarded as a person with "hang-ups" over issues of precedent and proper procedure. Because the purpose underlying the institution is truly important to you, others will see you as a hopeless idealist and "Goody Two-shoes." But because you believe in the standards and order required by a particular institution, you will also be seen as judgmental, noninclusive, an elitist defender of the status quo who lacks progressive values. In many parts of modern academia, your defense of institutional values, including the traditional rule of law, will be portrayed as siding with "the oppressor." And because your time horizon stretches generationally backward and forward, your colleagues currently on the scene will complain that you are not a team player.

Anyone who has read this far will recognize these to be misunderstandings, usually of a self-serving nature. But that will not prevent them from occurring. In fact, it ensures that they will constantly recur. Because institutional thinking has an inherently conserving quality, the most obvious source of misunderstanding and misrepresentation can be expected to come from the political left. However, in today's ideologically charged divisions in the political class you can also expect to run afoul of the political right. When results-oriented "conservatives" are not getting the partisan results they want, you can expect that you and your institutional values will be thrown overboard.

Fourth, if you are trying to think and act institutionally, you can expect to be taken advantage of. The reasons are obvious. Since playing by the rules matters to you, you can be outmaneuvered by self-seeking people who essentially care nothing for institutional rules. Since you really do believe in the aspirations of institutional purpose, you have opened yourself up to deception by cynics who can play on your loyalties. Since you are willing to persevere and suffer for the long-term good embodied in institutional values, other people can exploit your "high-mindedness" to their own advantage. It is in the nature of things that you will find yourself responsible to irresponsible people. Anyone inclined to regard these as abstract academic musings should reflect on the career of Colin Powell as a military officer and as U.S. secretary of state.[30]

Finally in this catalogue of dangers and costs, it is important to recognize that, while you must try not to be, you probably will be mostly alone. Let me begin to explain this rather elegiac thought.

Thinking institutionally is not a work of individual self-expression, though it does come down to the individual "I" who must do the thinking and acting. As I have tried to explain in Chapter 4, the institutionalist perspective amounts to an implicated life with others beyond the Self. Upholding institutional values is not something that can be in the head of just one person. And yet, to be an important practical force, institutional thinking also does not need to be in the heads of a great many people in a given organization or other larger setting. It takes a few people, regarding each other as more or less peers laboring for the common institutional cause, to keep one another straight and buck up the faltering colleague when the inevitable temptations of expediency and anti-institutional shortcuts arise. This is the truth behind Henri Stendhal's observation that one can acquire everything in solitude—except character.

The colleagues in question need not be alive to be part of "we few, we happy few, we band of brothers." In returning to several examples we have considered, it would seem that many if not most of the people in their "support group" for thinking institutionally were not alive. For the Chicago Cubs' Ryne Sandberg these people included the coaches who taught him the game and the old players "who paved the way for the rest of us." George Washington could gain needed support for his way of thinking from his brother, from his friend and neighbor George Mason, and a few others. But perhaps as important, there were also all of those dead heroes of the Roman Republic that he knew through plays and literature, above all Cato.[31] For his part, Madison seemed to draw lifelong strength from his old teachers Donald Robertson, John Witherspoon, and the Scottish Common Sense philosophers.

If people of that stature have needed the help of others, none of the rest of us are likely to get very far as loners pursuing some institutional cause. And yet the odds are that anyone trying to think and act institutionally today will have a great deal of difficulty finding many kindred spirits. An institutionalist can expect to spend a good deal of time paying the price that comes with "going it" mostly alone. Why should that be? Why is thinking institutionally so difficult and strangely isolating?

The Uphill Journey

We live in a time when thinking institutionally has become a countercultural act. Pursued with seriousness of purpose, institutional thinking amounts to a kind of subversive resistance movement against the prevailing trend of things. Obviously, this does not mean that protesters and counter-protesters are marching in the streets, some with placards shouting "Up with Institutions" and others proclaiming "Down with Institutions." What I mean is that anyone who tries to live out the "appreciative stance"—the internal point of view of institutional values—described in Chapter 4 will very quickly get a sense of struggling against powerful forces to the contrary. It all seems an unremitting uphill effort, and one has to wonder, why is this so?

To answer that question would, as academics like to say, require another book (and hopefully one more research grant). But more than just another book, it would require a vast depth of insight and breadth of scholarship. For that matter, it probably would also require the imaginative and expressive powers of a great poetic storyteller. None of that is on offer here.

The most I can hope to do is sketch the major forces that have been adding up to something crucial for the subject matter of this book. That "something" is a pervasive predisposition opposed to thinking and acting institutionally. By now, the momentum and mutually reinforcing quality of these forces have been at work for several centuries. If nothing else, surveying their cumulative impact should disabuse us of any notion that somehow we need to return to the "good old days" of respect and deference to the institutional authority of the powers that be. That is not a hope. It is a reactionary delusion giving up on the future. And institutionally minded persons truly do believe in the future. That is why they insist on investing in it.

Before summarizing the *longue durée* of these historical forces, we need to acknowledge the influence of practical circumstances. That is what hits us in the face every day. We will then go on to consider the deeper economic and political forces that have been working against a commitment to institutional values. Finally, we will try to take account of the powerful trends in intellectual culture that have been pushing in the same direction. The point of this little survey of such large topics is simply to indicate how a great many things have fit together to produce the particular result we now face in contemporary life. That result is to render institutional thinking ever more difficult and ever more necessary.

Things Practical

There are very practical reasons why faithful pursuit of institutional values is an uphill journey. As we have seen in earlier chapters, such values are intangible and elusive. They do not lend themselves to the social scientist's counting and measuring as a detached outsider observer. Institutional values require that a person give priority to elusive, long-term purposes and not to the first thing that comes to mind—namely, immediate gratification. Also, the pursuit of institutional values is demanding and costly, whereas we naturally want things to be easy and cheap.

Perhaps the greatest practical barrier is that thinking institution-ally asks us to serve something greater than ourselves.

These abstractions acquire force because there are so many surrounding pressures demanding short-term operational effec-tiveness. Misquoting T. S. Eliot, this is the shadow that falls between the thought and the action.[32] In our modern society, the standards and purposes of institutions usually have to be put into practice amid the operational imperatives of bureaucrati-cally structured organizations. Sheer administrative routine can attenuate and displace institutional thinking. Moreover, the modern organizations we inhabit have tasks that need to be accomplished now rather than later. Responding to what seems most urgent is likely to yield rewards, while delay in producing results invites criticism and punishment. Then too, in every walk of life there is a constant human temptation to abandon princi-ple and cut corners for the sake of various short-term personal advantages.

These are some of the realities of daily life that push us away from fidelity to institutional standards and purposes and toward quite understandable acts of expediency and opportunism. Any leader is especially vulnerable to these pressures, and nowhere is that truer than in the leadership of our political institutions. The comments of one recently disgraced politician go to the heart of the matter:

> From the time you arrive, the job of everybody in the office is about making you look good and feel good....The sun is rising with you—that's what everybody believes. You end up believing it too. The people in your office and the lobbyists, they're all saying the same thing: how great you are, and how hard you work for the state, and how much everybody appreciates you, and how you deserve to be rewarded. ... Somewhere around then is when the sense of entitlement takes over.[33]

Fortunately, most of the compromises of profession, office, and stewardship that people resort to are not of a criminal nature. However, it is also true that the little accommodations we make to expediency and opportunism are the ports of entry for what can become larger betrayals of institutional purpose. Turning back to the scandal chronicle in Box 2.1, if we could know the full story behind any entry, we would probably find it begins with some seemingly harmless accommodation of that nature.

These practical obstacles to institutional thinking might be called the force of circumstance. They represent a kind of friction in everyday life that works against any effort actually to do what this book is commending.

However, lying behind the force of circumstance are much larger historical developments. These developments have more actively worked against people's adopting and holding on to an institutional outlook. In order to understand our current situation we need at least briefly to take these economic, political, and cultural forces into account. Again, my purpose is not to say anything new but to identify the ensemble of factors that have combined to make institutional thinking so difficult today. This ensemble is impressive but it need not be discouraging. Powerful as these forces have been in the past several centuries, they have not been able to subdue that inward wisdom of everyday life, the place where, half-consciously perhaps, we cherish institutional values.

Things Economical

The first part of this historical ensemble is the economic system we have come to take for granted. Developing over the last three to four centuries, it is the way our modern society expects—and as a practical matter demands—that human beings will work, produce, and consume. It can be called industrial capitalism, whereby some people use money to make money and other people sell their labor for wages. It can be called the "market revolution," in which the impersonal exchange mechanism to buy, sell, and commodify sweeps through anything in its path. It can be called the growth of a new commercial civilization, virtually all of whose social relationships are technically rationalized to facilitate mass production and consumption.

These and many other characterizations might be applied to the economic way of life we now take for granted. It is an economic system that no one planned (although political economists like Adam Smith and Karl Marx could brilliantly explicate it), and it has fed on itself. Despite all the ups and downs and withering criticisms directed against it, the capitalist, market-driven, commercial economy is a system that has worked. It has worked in the sense of generally yielding the ever-growing material benefits people want for themselves and their families.

For our purposes, what matters are the implications for thinking and acting institutionally. The term "creative destruction" has been used to characterize the way in which this modern system of economic growth operates, and it is a useful concept to describe the impact of this system on institutions.

Observers have had little trouble identifying what this modern way of economic life destroys. It destroys traditional societies and their institutions. Since the first land enclosures in England began paving the way for commercial agriculture and eventual industrialization, poets and commoners alike have been lamenting the loss of "the old ways" brought on by economic modernization.[34] Obviously, this story has not ended. The intrinsic features of a market economy's operations are a continuous assault on established institutional relationships, unless those relationships can somehow be shaped to the demands of the economic marketplace. The growing mobility of capital and human resources undermines enduring community ties. What is local, particular, and face-to-face succumbs to what is standardized, universal, and impersonal. What cannot be bought or sold is devalued.

As far as institutions are concerned, the "creative" part of creative destruction is also clear. The modern market economy replaces the informal, long-standing institutions of traditional society with formally rationalized bureaucratic "institutions" designed for operational efficiency. It is a rich irony. The more passionate the love of money has grown in industrial society, the more dispassionate and methodical its forms of life have had to become. Sixty years before Max Weber systematized the study of bureaucracy, Alexis de Tocqueville observed that "though industry often brings in its train great disorders and great disasters, it cannot prosper without exceedingly regular habits and the performance of a long succession of small uniform motions. The more lively the passion, the more regular and uniform must these motions be."[35] Thus an organization of human relationships that had been socially organic gives way to organizations that are purely technical and instrumental in quality. These are the places where modern people can expect to spend most of their lives.

Obviously, this did not happen all at once. Well through the nineteenth century, the dominant voices in America's rapidly industrializing economy continued to portray the modern capitalists' overturning of traditional society as nothing more than a reaffirmation of traditional values. They could do so because their Protestant heritage had endorsed hard work at a worldly calling as a sign of godliness. The happy result for the new captains of industry was a combination of social status achieved by rabid devotion to profit-making (which traditional societies denigrated) together with claims to the moral high ground based on traditional character values, such as thrift, enterprise, and self-denial.

However, by the twentieth century, the momentum of economic modernization was overturning that position as well. The individual capitalist-owner-manager gave way to the rise of the modern corporation and professionalized bureaucracies. Calls to thrift, self-denial, and deferred gratification became relics of the past. What businessmen were learning by the beginning of the twentieth century was that the big money was to be made on the other side of the tracks. Their calling was to feed and, through all the modern arts of mass persuasion, encourage an endless appetite for the consumption of goods and services. And if that means "no money down," so much the better.

In the process just sketched, it became natural for people to identify mere organizations—especially the rationalized bureaucratic structures that pervade our lives—with institutions. (That is why we had to take pains at the outset of Chapter 4 to distinguish the two.) This conflation of institutions with the large-scale bureaucracies of production and modern life in general could render anti-institutionalism a good thing in popular thinking. Resisting organized institutions was a way of battling for the preservation of the human spirit. For example, at the beginning of the twentieth century the popular historian John Ridpath wrote volumes that, though forgotten now, graced the parlors of many an upwardly mobile middle-class family. Ending the ninth volume of his *World History,* he observed: "Mankind have been organized to death. . . . Among all the civil, political, and churchly institutions of the world, it would be difficult today to select that one which is not in a large measure conducted in the interest of the official management. The Organization has become the principal thing, and the Man only a secondary consideration."[36]

It's a short lane that knows no turnings, and what Ridpath could not perceive was that the modern market economy was just in the process of turning itself into a vast machine for selling the common man on the idea that he and his immediate wants are indeed "the principal thing." The more the cultural avant-garde of modern artists and intellectual radicals insisted that the institutional structure of bourgeois values must be overturned, the more adept the market economy became at capitalizing on this desire for personal self-fulfillment. As if in quicksand, struggling for personal freedom and self-expression further immersed a person in a world of things and experiences to buy as a way to achieve that self-fulfillment.

To take an extreme example, before the twentieth century the quest for romantic love was generally perceived as a threat to the established order. It was an untamed passion that elevated the irrational desires of individuals over the demands of any settled institutions. But in the early twentieth century, romantic love began a process of becoming tamed and commodified.[37] This most intimate form of self-expression soon lost its religious and tragic overtones in favor of a vision of personal happiness portrayed throughout popular fiction, advertisements, and the new technologies of film and radio entertainment. The new rituals of romance might be outside the normal institutional routines of work and home, but they are not outside the demands of the market economy. They require certain forms of consumption—travel, dining out, expensive gifts, entertainment, as well as buying various kinds of clothing, personal accessories, body products, diet plans, and, alas, gym memberships.

Our modern economic system is a massive historical force, and it leaves the twenty-first century institutionalist in a double bind. On the one hand, all things institutional carry the stigma associated with the bureaucratic-rationalized-organizational way of living through which the whole system operates. We experience "the institutional" as personally stultifying. On the other hand, the same economic system caters to and constantly teaches a short-term, self-centered ethic of personal gratification. This view is incessantly marketed as the standard by which to judge what is personally fulfilling, thus working against institutional thinking from the other end.

Meanwhile, the modern market economy continues its work of dissolving institutional loyalties. Contrary to expectations of many economists earlier in the twentieth century, we now know that the modern market economy does not mature into forms of settled relationships. On the contrary, it is a dynamic force demanding ever greater adaptability and complexity in people's lives.[38] On the consumption side, it is in the system's self-interest to create appetites that can never be satisfied and always stand poised to switch to the next new thing. On the production side, the same self-interest demands that economic organizations show little real loyalty to the people who are working for them. In the modern firm's striving for operational efficiency and effectiveness, everyone and everything must be ultimately disposable. Because of their higher salaries, retirement benefits, and health costs, employees with a long-term commitment to the organization can appear as little more than a financial drain on the bottom line. Not surprisingly, today's workers have realized that to survive, they must reciprocate with the same lack of institutional loyalty.

Things Political

The second great force weighing in against institutional thinking in our times is political. It is that ongoing historical phenomenon that Alexis de Tocqueville in the 1830s simply called "democracy." Broadly understood, democracy is the sea we all swim in today. That is why we can hardly even notice as its current carries us in certain directions. However, the fact is that the democratic current is continuously pushing against the possibility of thinking and acting institutionally.

Tocqueville recognized that democracy was not just a way of governing but also a way of life that was coming to dominate the modern world. It grew out of a historical process that, despite the centuries of advance and retreat, kept adding up to a new understanding of human affairs. It was what Tocqueville called the ongoing commitment to equality of condition—no one better than anyone else but everybody as good as anyone else. America had escaped the horrific struggles for democratic equality in European history and had a relatively fresh slate as its point of departure in this larger movement. Because America was "born democratic," as he put it, one could see all the implications of democracy especially clearly in this young nation.

In terms of our interests in this book, Tocqueville describes a number of tendencies promoted by democracy that make thinking institutionally an uphill battle. They match up nicely with the feature of a market economy that we have just discussed. One such political tendency is the foreshortening of time horizons. A democratic age disrespects the past for an obvious reason. It has been able to come into existence only by breaking with the hereditary claims of monarchy and aristocracy. Its forward movement depends on asserting the rights of the people against the dead hand of the past. Traditions are easily interpreted as impositions on the freedom of equal individuals to make their own choices. Inherited formalities are despised as useless impediments to the immediate fulfillment of democratic desires. In the turmoil of an ever churning society of equal individuals, what matters is what is new. By the same token, with change always in the air and sudden gain and loss everywhere, "the present looms large and hides the future, so that men do not want to think beyond tomorrow." People have a fear of long-term obligations. "and they are right to feel this fear, for in ages of democracy all things are unstable, but the most unstable of all is the human heart."[39] Interestingly enough, as Tocqueville was back in France in 1833 beginning to write his book about the United States, former president John Quincy Adams was confiding to his diary: "Democracy has no forefathers, it looks to no posterity, it is swallowed up in the present and thinks of nothing but itself."[40]

The second relevant tendency is democracy's pressure to shrink people's vision of values into predominantly material categories. Obliterated are the distinctions among people based on birth, social status, occupation, and all the other rankings that dominate a predemocratic society. In their place looms the one dominant distinction based on money. Tocqueville discerns that the passion for moneymaking is not because democratic people have narrower souls "but because money really is more important" in democratic societies. For example, in traditional societies tenants pay rents to landlords not only in the form of money and goods but also by exchanges of respect, attachment, and service. In democracy's landlord/tenant relationship, money alone is paid, and all other obligations are nonexistent. In a democratic society, with no one owing service to anyone else based on social rankings, tradition, and the like, everything you want must be paid for. "This infinitely multiplies the purpose to which wealth may be applied and increases its value."[41]

Nor does democracy celebrate and drive aspirations toward just any kind of wealth. In democracy it is largely the wealth acquired by a passion for moneymaking that matters. With aristocratic privileges overturned in democratic societies, old money is never secure. Gone too are the possibilities of accumulating wealth through the old aristocratic regime's resort to war, public employment, and political confiscations of property. Moneymaking must occur through industry, risk-taking, and individual effort. To his credit, Tocqueville did foresee the danger of an industrial aristocracy of wealth emerging over time, which is exactly what happened by the end of the nineteenth century. He had no way of imagining the vast wealth now obtainable through high-tech war, political favors, and government contracting in the modern U.S. democracy. But for our purposes that is beside the point. Tocqueville accurately discerned the main line of development. Democracy would focus on immediate material payoffs over larger, nonmonetized values.

That main line of development amounts to a strong head current against institutional thinking. Just as the foreshortening of time horizons works against intergenerational obligations, democracy's moneymaking ethic works against "an infusion of value beyond the task at hand." It does so by disparaging commitments to the nonmaterial quality of institutional values. Any would-be institutionalist is cast into the role of either an impractical visionary or an elitist taking on airs about office and stewardship. And of course a devotion to moneymaking and material success indirectly denigrates the institutionalist's claim that there are things of great value that cannot be bought or sold. In short, upholding the humane purposes of institutions is not likely to measure up to the democratic standard of monetarily "making it" in the "real world."

In the third place, democracy gives a ringing endorsement to the assertion, not the subordination, of the individual self. This view of the priority of the individual and the individual's personal judgment aligns neatly with what we will shortly discuss as "things philosophical." But as Tocqueville makes clear, this outlook—the individual's lone judgment "as the most apparent and accessible test of truth"—derives from democracy itself, not from reading works of philosophy. Indeed, "of all the countries in the world, America is the one in which the precepts of Descartes are least studied and best followed."[42]

Tocqueville saw that democratic equality sets its face against not only the hierarchy of traditional society but also all received authority one has not chosen for oneself. This attitude is associated with many things we rightly cherish about the American spirit. It expresses and fosters a love of liberty among people who insist on their individual right to choose their own way in "the pursuit of happiness." It emphasizes personal initiative, independence, and responsibility. It is the democratic attitude that helped produce a vibrant religious scene among individuals who believe in the right to think for oneself.

At the same time, assertion of the democratic self makes it difficult to learn and appreciate the ways of institutional thinking. Equality, Tocqueville said, makes men independent of one another and inclined to follow nobody's will but their own. The result we see around us is a predisposition to treat our political and social relationships in largely "contractual" terms. Legitimate institutional arrangements are those that are freely chosen and controlled by autonomous individuals, a mutually advantageous bargain among the contracting parties and little more. That is not the same thing as being anti–institutional, but it is a thinned-out, fragile version of participation in the life and purposes of institutions. In democratic society "free institutions" (in the sense of voluntary civic associations) flourish, and that is all to the good, given the tendency toward rampant individualism. But they flourish as transient exchanges of convenience rather than deep institutional commitments. Their easily revocable affiliations are a veneer of "institutional" activity that should not be mistaken for the basic and more demanding institutional hardwood. To be sure, institutions rightly understood exist for people and not vice versa. But as I also argued earlier, thinking institutionally does require a subordination of self-assertion to institutional purposes of a public nature.[43] This is not the kind of character that democracy tends to produce over time. The self-promoting figures we see on today's reality television shows do not appear to be the sort of people you would want to depend on to build and sustain important institutions.

From the political realm of democracy comes a final tendency making institutional thinking an uphill journey. It appears to contradict what we have just said about self-assertion, but as Tocqueville showed so well, it does not. Since in democratic times people are equal and independent of one another, they are also individually weak in confronting their democratic society. Any one of the millions of little democratic figures engaged in asserting its self is as nothing in the face of those millions taken together in asserting itself as majority opinion. Majoritarianism is another name for the democratic majority's adoration of itself. And in the light of that adoration, the spirit of the groveling courtier is put within the reach of millions of individuals.

How this relates to our subject should be clear. Institutions are intermediary bodies—more than the sum of self-asserting individuals but less than the monolithic whole of society. Institutionalists know that particular institutions, their values and purposes, are not tools for the immediate gratification of majorities. But that is exactly what the impatient, self-worshiping democratic majority and its courtiers typically want. Institutional thinking insists on a mature, well-balanced view of institutional loyalty, or if you like, a grownup's view of office. I believe it is true that in thinking and acting institutionally a person can find constructive refuge. It is refuge from the vulnerability of the lone individual's assertive self-life that Alexis de Tocqueville foresaw in the future of democratic man. But it also true that a person taking such refuge will always be engaged in a defensive effort to protect any given institution from the incessant, short-term pressures of majority opinion. The uphill road comes with the democratic territory.

Things Philosophical

For almost five centuries now, intellectual currents in the West have been beating against what this book calls institutional thinking. We are still living on the growing edge of that development. What can one say about this? It would be ridiculous to try to offer a full account here. But it would be irresponsible, a dereliction of duty in such a book, to say nothing at all about this intellectual legacy. There are powerful, intellectually structured forces that simply must be pointed out, even if we can do so only in passing. Otherwise, the current pressures against institutional thinking will seem far too mysterious.

What some have called "the making of the modern mind" has been to a large degree the making of an anti-institutionalist mind. If we want to understand why thinking institutionally is so difficult and strangely isolating today, philosophical currents have to be added to the ensemble of economic and political forces. Before today's academic leaders could be able to define liberal education in our elite universities as a project for "unsettling, defamiliarizing, disorienting, and inducing alienation" among students, there has to have been an erosion of something deeper in the Western consciousness. In things philosophical there has been erosion and loss but also creation and gain. The following comments are not intended to judge whether the overall result has been a net gain or loss in human affairs. We will leave that to the combatants in the so-called culture war. What I do want to point out is the immense challenge that modern intellectual developments pose to anyone today who aspires to think and act institutionally.

Charles Taylor has persuasively described "the modern identity" in terms of a particular sense of self.[44] It is a self defined by powers of both disengaged reason and creative imagination. It is a self committed both to unencumbered individual autonomy and to the shared moral standards embodied in rights, human freedom, and equal dignity. As modern people we aspire to the ideals of individual expression and self-fulfillment while also endorsing the demands for universal benevolence and justice. This modern identity is pervasive, but it is built up from different strands of older and newer ways of thinking. Taylor describes at length these diverse moral sources and how they coexist like tensioned historical strata shaping what we see on the surface. Partisans of different components attack each other—the instrumental reason of the Enlightenment versus the expressive emotionalism of the Romantic Movement—and never seem to realize that as moderns their identity is participating in all these components.

At risk of appearing paranoid, I think it can be said that virtually all of the major intellectual components making up our modern identity have helped, both individually and in combination, to undermine the institutional perspective presented in this book. The three major movements doing this work are oversimplified with the terms the Enlightenment, Romanticism, and Modernism, but we will stick with those conventional labels.

In recent years scholars have emphasized that "the" Enlightenment was not a single doctrinaire "project." It was plural—a multifaceted process occurring in different places throughout Western Europe and the English colonies in the eighteenth century and even earlier.[45] However, for our purposes the important thing is that there were central tendencies and ideas held in common in this ongoing process that are crucial to our modern anti–institutionalist outlook.

As Immanuel Kant famously put it in 1784, to be enlightened is to have the maturity and courage to use your own understanding and not be guided by another.

The model of intelligence was not to be a learned recipient of anything. It was to be open-minded, to doubt, suspend judgment, and continuously inquire. Reason itself requires that nothing be accepted on authority, that everything be questioned, analyzed, and reconstructed in the light of intelligence. The only doctrine of the enlightened person is to have no "doctrine" and to take the best of what reason and experience show you.

The Enlightenment's *philosophe* was a new kind of philosopher, an independent, humanistic person of letters appealing to public opinion (which was thus being enlightened by the *philosophe's* very appeal to it) and not to political rulers and church authorities of traditional society. As Denis Diderot's magisterial *Encyclopedia* put it, a *philosophe* is a person who, "trampling on prejudice, tradition, universal consent, authority, in a word all that enslaves most minds, dares to think for himself ...[and] to admit nothing except on the testimony of his experience and his reason." Enlightenment philosophy was "the organized habit of criticism."[46]

In this view, the free play of critical inquiry is especially a matter of liberating people from all those things of the past—superstitions, ignorant traditions, self-serving authorities, and institutions—that have hitherto encumbered their thinking. Educated to use their own minds, free people can discover and follow the rules of conduct existing in the laws that govern both physical and human nature, for nature is reason in action. By his own reason and observation of the world, every individual possesses within himself the means for attaining true knowledge. A thinking person is not subservient to the authority of tradition or masters. Certain knowledge is that knowledge you can be sure of because you yourself are the judge. As we saw earlier, this is a "philosophy" that came naturally to democracy, with every man his own *philosophe*.

Criticism's destructive work had a positive purpose. With the ground cleared of superstition, prejudice, and received opinion, man's reason could lead to ever-advancing improvements in the human condition on earth. Some Enlightenment thinkers launched a radical assault on the authority of the Christian religion, both its institutional structures and its "magical thinking." However, the *philosophe's* hopes of replacing the traditional view of God with nature and reason were mostly suppressed during the one hundred years prior to the onset of the French Revolution. The larger intellectual movement was much more successful in arguing that religious authorities and traditional God talk should simply be sidelined in favor of focusing on the use of human reason to better man's condition in this world. The goal of reason was progress—advancing human happiness in the here and now. Here science and freedom would work together. Freed from religious and philosophical authorities of the past, science was now racing forward. This greater mastery of nature in turn provided unprecedented human freedom to control nature for man's benefit (for example, through inoculations and other medical treatments, scientific land management, animal breeding, and public health measures).

Just as rational control of the physical world would increase mankind's happiness, so too would rational understanding and engineering of his sociopolitical world. The reasoning faculties and practices that were bringing revolutionary understandings of the physical realm would do the same in man's social existence. With the spread of enlightened thinking among people, things standing in the way of human happiness could be overcome by continued critical application of human reason to experience. The old institutional regime of inherited privilege, oppression, and cruelty would be replaced with new, rational ways of conducting human affairs. Thus as the present age was more enlightened than the past, subsequent ages of human society would continue to progress through applications of man's natural faculties of reason and observation.

But again, this bright future for humanity depended on rejecting the encumbrances of the past and external authorities. Observing and describing how the world actually works, natural sciences were making astonishing new discoveries because they had thrown off the dead hand of past philosophical and theological authorities saying how nature ought to work. So, too, there must be a new science of human affairs that declares and describes what men do and really are, not what they ought to do and should be. The moralizing of traditionalists needed to be replaced with "social science." Although Enlightenment thinking did not have that latter term, it had taken the essential step in that direction. It was not a matter of cynicism but of careful observation by disengaged reason to see that virtue was an idea created to mask the true motives of human selfishness, a "vice" that actually turned out to be of public benefit.[47] Among other things, political science, economics, and sociology were in the process of being born.

Today's institutionalist, taking faithful reception from the past, should be grateful for what "the" Enlightenment as a multifaceted process has handed down to us. The institutionalist does so with a quality of appreciation that Enlightenment thinkers themselves denied to those whose work they freely inherited and exploited, not least the critical work of Medieval and Renaissance Christian scholars.[48] Be that as it may, we today should appreciate that the Enlightenment infused into the modern identity respect for the individual, a commitment to tolerance and free inquiry, and a ringing endorsement of the equal natural rights and liberties of all human beings. Not least, Enlightenment thinkers set in motion an ongoing political program insisting that the well-being of individual human beings was the purpose of "good" institutions.

However, long-run forces undermining institutional values were also set in motion. For one thing, in their careless dismissal of the past, Enlightenment thinkers encouraged subsequent generations to forget how heavily their enlightened insight was drawing on—as well as distorting—the philosophical and religious intellectual resources of past centuries. The wisdom of the past was both plundered and recklessly discounted.

Next, the Enlightenment's "uncritical" confidence in the power of human reason consistently denigrated the habits and institutional loyalties of ordinary life. Anything engrained in institutions was simply an impediment to the freedom of individuals and societies to create their desired future. In other words, Enlightenment thinking sought to annul man's finiteness. The partial understandings accessible to the human mind were now proudly proclaimed to be the fullness of man's meaning in history. Man himself would provide for the consummation of history. In so claiming to release individuals from all forms of necessity and limitation, the Enlightenment unleashed currents of thought hostile to any concern for the stability, continuity, and even meaningfulness of established institutions. Reason's aspiration for heaven on earth turned into messianic political yearnings for total revolution. It produced that striving for abstract, institutional-less individuals and for social utopias to which institutional thinking, as we discussed earlier, is utterly opposed. When institutional attachments are equated with chains and ignorance, human beings are not on their way to being free. They are on their way to being lost.

From here other anti-institutionalist forces were set in motion. The Enlightenment's optimistic view of reason and human nature refused to acknowledge that each level of historic achievement brings its own corruptions and contradictions. It carelessly disregarded an older wisdom teaching that each enhancement in human powers increases possibilities for evil as well as for good.[49] Given the flawed human materials with which it must work, this faith in progress has inevitably led to disappointment, especially in the twentieth century. It has produced disillusionment, despair, and cultural defeatism. This, too, has worked against institutional thinking. As we have seen, such thinking is grounded in belief in a future of limited, partial, but immensely valuable institutional purposes that are worth working for, day in and day out, under the obligations of profession, office, and stewardship.

Then, too, the Enlightenment's faith in disengaged reason brought with it an inherent instrumentalism. It views the world as so much physical material available to serve the purposes of human intellect. This has encouraged an instrumental approach to making and remaking institutions at will. There are no grounds for human humility, no mysteries that the intellect cannot fathom. What matters is the use-value of things and people. This utilitarian outlook became embedded in the bureaucratic institutions of the modern market economy. Such elements of Enlightenment thinking (Rousseau comes to mind) could then be exploited to justify sacrificing individual rights for the sake of the general good.

In protest against all this, the counterforce of Romanticism launched its own attack on institutional thinking. Now it was self-expression and creative imagination rather than reason that were given primacy. Nature was seen to possess an inner richness with which the individual heart and spirit could unite. At least during the early stages of the nineteenth-century Romantic Movement, opening oneself to the epiphany of these deeper harmonies was seen to produce a spontaneous morality and benevolence.

Seen from this viewpoint, institutions only get in the way of what is most truly human. Their authority represents a denial of individual self-expression and creativity. Their fixed givenness contradicts the human freedom that requires portable roots. And to be sure, this critique would only become more salient as industrialization, urbanization, and modern bureaucracies expanded during and after the nineteenth century. The necessary mode of existence in a capitalist technological society could persuasively be depicted as suffocating people's humanity, their sympathies toward each other, and their harmony with nature. Modern institutions now appeared spiritless and passionless. At their best, they are nothing more than the carriers of a smug and hypocritical bourgeois morality.

Thus the drive for self-fulfillment has reinforced the anti-institutional bias of rationalistic instrumentalism. In other words, the contending parties on both sides—the Enlightenment versus the Romantic movements—have produced a common verdict as regards institutions. Institutions are carriers of cultural authority—of orthodoxy—and as such are cast as the inherent enemy of human vitality and genius. Institutional authority is the enemy of reason as regards the Enlightenment and of self-expression as regards the Romantic revolt against the Enlightenment. Either way, the institutionalist perspective is devalued and dismissed. In this intellectual environment the best it can hope for is to slink away from the scene of its various crimes.

This sketch of things philosophical carries us through the end of the nineteenth century. Modernism then became another layer added to the contemporary outlook. Artists led the way in this revolt against established institutional values, and others in our culture soon followed. The authentic self is one engaged in a ceaseless exploration of experience and new sensibilities. In this mission, all forms and boundaries must be broken down in searching out new sensations and identities. The task is to "reflect" nothing, for to do so is to be part of the dead past. The task is to "express" everything about oneself and embrace what is continually new. Only then is a person on the way to realizing his or her full, unique potential. That is the only thing one can truly hope to have and to hold.

Events more than philosophical arguments have driven Modernism and its offspring. Modern artists saw through the contentions of Enlightenment and Romantic thinking because that was the only way of making sense of things in the early twentieth century and the horrors of World War I. Events revealed the existing political and social institutions of the pre-war years to be merciless and incompetent. They had tricked people into deference. By the 1920s the intellectual leaders of Western culture had at least one common theme: the only thing traditional institutions deserve, and richly so, is abandonment.

Since then, the incessant message from modern literature and the arts has been that institutions are not something to which authentic, free, and savvy individuals should want to be attached. There is a phony and diabolical "churchiness" about them. They crush the individual's aesthetic aspiration for life. Their moral standards are likely to be incompatible with personal fulfillment. And again an irony of anti-institutionalism repeats itself. In their rebellion against established forms and fascination with the new, modernists and postmodernists fit in nicely with the modern market economy's hostility to traditionalism. Likewise, the Modernist striving for freedom from all sources of obligation extrinsic to the human will makes for a very willing consumer.

Various human potential movements have been encouraged by the Romantic and Modernist currents of thought. Such self-help movements have flourished in modern times, and no doubt many individuals have benefited as a result. For our purposes, however, the important point is that this flourishing has further undercut the moral sources for institutional thinking. The reason is that with expressive fulfillment and self-realization as the ultimate criteria, larger moral purposes tend to dissolve. Claims of obligation beyond the self are now interpreted as arbitrariness and mere power plays of dominant social and political interests. Loyalty to institutional values and purposes is naive submission to the powers that be. In this now dominant modern perspective, moral commitments are a matter of emoting one's purely subjective feelings about "values."

And ironically enough, this modern expression of Romantic subjectivism has simply served to reinforce the prevailing trends it opposes. With the good reduced to personal preferences and feelings, modern thinkers have been left with procedural fairness as the only working standard for interpersonal judgments. But at this point the search for meaning degenerates into the celebration of empty process. I champion your and everyone else's right to speak out, but there is no real reason I should listen to you. When the utilitarian ethic of procedural fairness becomes the sole normative standard, the self-expressive modern counterculture has simply fitted itself into the instrumentalist, bureaucratic world of procedures that it claims to challenge.[50]

And So the Uphill Climb

In very general terms, I have tried to summarize the forces that make it such an uphill, often thankless climb for anyone trying to think institutionally today. For roughly twenty generations, a series of economic, political, and intellectual movements have been working their way through Western society. They have amounted to a thoroughgoing onslaught against institutional values and commitments. With each passing generation these forces have made it more difficult to be institutionally minded. That is why today such thinking amounts to a countercultural act. A mentality that is roughly the opposite of thinking institutionally has been absorbed into the marrow of academic and popular culture, as well as everything in between. Enjoy the show but don't be taken in. Believe whatever you like, but trust nothing. Institutions are both empty formalities we can make and remake at will, and also oppressive juggernauts crushing the human spirit. From the assertion of human autonomy it is only a short step to a preoccupation with self and individual success, and from there another short step to the failures of ethical leadership we see in institutions all around us.

Amid all of this, the institutionalist can seem a hapless moralist. The conservative hates decomposition and the radical celebrates it. By contrast the institutionalist is engaged in trying to turn things toward a recomposition that will carry forward the best of the past into the future. This is the respect-in-depth that characterizes his or her uphill exertions. The institutionalist seeks a sane way to keep pursuing aspirations for the good of human beings as those ends are expressed in institutional purposes and values.

In writing about the dangers of and obstacles to institutional thinking, it might appear I am arguing the whole subject of this book into oblivion. Given the immense opposing forces, the uphill journey can appear to be a fool's errand. Rather than the myth of Sisyphus, who pushed the stone uphill each day only to find it back at the bottom the next morning, it might seem more like a tale of Sisyphus's dumber brother, who finds the stone rolling back on him every time he pushes it.

But there is no need to buy into this gloomy image. A more realistic view of our situation would find its likeness in *Pilgrim's Progress*. Pilgrim's way is one of trial and struggle. But it is also a path of deep satisfaction because he is struggling for what is of immense, enduring value. His is an ennobling journey because it is not just uphill but upward toward something better.

Similarly, I have suggested throughout this book that institutionalists can be found making their way in many places. We encounter them in the history books about a Washington, Madison, and Lincoln. We find them in the news stories about whistleblowers doing their duty amid political and business scandals, and about sports figures who really do play with respect for the game. Beyond that, we can recognize a more or less institutional frame of mind in the various encounters of daily life—in offices, garages, stores, schoolrooms, and all the rest. Sometimes we can recognize it in a part of ourselves. To be sure, the encounters are not as often as we might like, but we do recognize them when they occur. No one has to tell us that this institutional *habitas,* or bent of disposition, is pushing us toward doing things in an appropriate manner. These recognitions are not relics destined for oblivion. They are witnesses pointing toward a better way.

Our distrust of institutions is not going to go away. By now it is deeply entwined in our modern culture's genetic code. But it is not so much distrust as cynicism that threatens us individually in our personal lives and collectively as a functioning society. Hence the counsel: distrust but value. We may well distrust institutionalized organizations and those people who would abuse their power. But we can still value the humane purposes of "good" institutions, especially the superintending institutions of law and government that all the others depend on. We can work at thinking and acting institutionally in the business of daily life. And we can take genuine satisfaction doing so in light of all the shortsighted, self-serving, and destructive pressures to the contrary.

To live in a world of nothing but institutional thinking would be a monstrosity. By the same token, to live in a world in which institutional thinking is absent, or so heavily discounted as to fade into insignificance—that, too, would be a monstrosity. So is it all a wash? Hardly. The danger in our times is not too much but too little institutional thinking. That is why the preceding discussion of dangers and uphill obstacles can so readily seem to push the subject of this book downward into oblivion. Oblivion is the place where you do not even know there is something to worry about. We can never recognize the danger posed by the growing incapacity for institutional thinking unless we have some way of talking about something that risks being forgotten. That is why I began by saying that this book is an effort at recovery and articulation on behalf of an unfashionable idea. That has to be the first step since, as the poet Czeslaw Milosz wrote, "What is pronounced strengthens itself. What is not pronounced tends to nonexistence."[51]

CHAPTER SIX
WAYS OF THINKING,
WAYS OF BEING

The preceding chapter took as its point of departure an obvious fact: it is possible to think without acting. You and I may treat "thinking institutionally" as an interesting intellectual exercise and still never do anything about it. Yet while it is possible to think without acting, it is not possible to act without thinking.

To that statement, the natural first response might be, "What nonsense." We see people acting without thinking all the time. It is the sort of behavior that makes up the bulk of the daily news 365 days a year. Only an academic in some tower of ivory could claim it is impossible to act without thinking. So let me try to clarify what I mean.

By saying it is not possible to act without thinking I am not referring to responses of a person's autonomic nervous system, like jumping at the sound of an unexpected loud noise or unconsciously breathing in and out. By "act" I mean making a conscious move in the world. That includes acting on impulse, or as we often say, "without time to think." Such situations are especially revealing of our deeper thought patterns. When we do not have "time to think" and can only respond based on what is already in the character of our mental outlook—that is when our thinking, our foundational thinking, is most clearly exposed.

I am not trying to say something obscure or academically clever. Anyone who has ever been romantically involved with another person knows that what I am saying is true. If you want to know what the person you are dating is really about, do not study what is going on during the dating ritual. Pay attention to what happens when the person thinks no one else is watching. And pay special attention as this person responds to the unexpected. To put the point crudely, watch a person's "gut" response in order to get a reading on what is going on in his or her head. The ancient wisdom literature expresses it more elegantly: As a person "thinks in his heart, so is he" and "out of it [your heart] are the issues of life" (Proverbs 23:7; 4:23). We act in the way we think deep down at the heart level. You and I may not be what we think we are, but what we think, we are.

In Chapter 4 I tried to describe what it is like to inhabit and move around in a particular frame of mind called "institutional." And throughout this book I have pressed the case for reviving and living out this normative point of view. As I said at the outset, thinking institutionally is nothing dramatic, new, or flashy. It is more like revisiting a forgotten old home place and experiencing a re-cognition—a bringing to mind again—of valuable things that only appear to have been forgotten. The discussion has tried to focus on background presumptions about right relationships. As best I can, I have tried to describe a "respect-in-depth" way of thinking about our lives and surroundings.

By contrast, thanks to modern communication technology, virtually everything we are now lured to pay attention to focuses on fleeting foreground features and short-lived personal encounters. The Internet and its related technologies have given almost everyone something that is unique in human history— the means for indiscriminate self-expression, and this in a "virtual" world where nothing really endures or has substance. The allure of the ephemeral is now enveloping us, and it seems destined to do nothing but grow.[1]

In such times it makes excellent sense both to distrust and to value institutions—to distrust because institutional purposes are pursued through the actions of flawed human beings, and to value because institutions have enduring purposes worthy of our efforts and loyalties. Thinking institutionally is about using our reason. However, it pushes a person to go beyond being instrumentally rational—that is, simply making intelligent choices regarding means to some arbitrary and self-validating goals we happen to have chosen simply to please ourselves. It calls on a substantive rationality regarding intelligent choices about the ends of action worth choosing.

The rational basis for evaluating institutions is not a matter of personal whim. The basis is the good any given institution produces for human well-being. The deep-seated purposes of institutions are aspirations in that upward direction. Those are aspirations to which we can appropriately hold ourselves accountable. In a perplexing world, they can orient the modern search for "authenticity" in our individual life commitments. They can help us discern the limits of loyalty to any particular organization or process, though they can never shield us from the agony of having to make hard choices.

Is it really so difficult to cut through the fluff and blather of our popular culture to see the things that need to be taught and learned? The chronicle of misdeeds discussed at the beginning of this book points toward the immense gains to be had from thinking institutionally. Those gains are both societal and personal in nature.

At the most basic level, there is the matter of sustainability and survival. We noted an elemental form of institutional thinking that consists of not critically questioning everything you are doing and simply carrying on with your job as it is supposed to be done. If nothing else, the steady habits in such thinking (not the same thing as addictive behavior) have immense survival value for society at large. They give implicit testimony to and support for the value of the going concern of the social order. The multitude of nameless people who are—in Ryne Sandberg's phrase—"just doing what I'm supposed to do" amounts to an immense sheet anchor sustaining civilized life, something we never are likely to notice until disaster strikes.

History offers compelling examples of societies surviving through devastating cataclysms by virtue of ordinary people simply carrying on with their appointed duties. A historian has described the similar grounds of social survival in the atomic bombing of Japan and the Black Death in fourteenth-century Europe:

> In the worst years of the mortality, Europeans witnessed horrors comparable to Hiroshima and Nagasaki, but even when death was everywhere and only a fool would dare to hope, the thin fabric of civilization held....Enough notaries, municipal and church authorities, physicians and merchants stepped forward to keep governments and courts and churches and financial houses running—albeit at a much reduced level.[2]

In ordinary times as well, institutional thinking holds great value on a variety of fronts. It injects a concern for something more than the claims of personal power and temporary advantage. With at least some people around you who are thinking institutionally, there is a greater chance of being told what you need to hear rather than simply what you want to hear. Institutional thinking also helps protect against the willful ignorance called presentism—the arrogant privileging of one's own little moment in time. Institutional thinking transforms the past into memory, which is a way of keeping alive what is meaningful in the qualitative significance of our experiences. Because it is attentive to rule-following rather than personal strategies to achieve personal ends, thinking institutionally enhances predictability in conduct. Predictability in turn can enhance trust, which can enhance reciprocating loyalty, which can facilitate bargaining, compromise, and fiduciary relationships. All this is a chain of relationships that amounts to a civilized way for people to live together.

In the end, the advantages of institutional thinking come down to what is distinctly human. Humans flourish through attachments to authoritative communities, not as totally unencumbered selves. Because institutional thinking goes beyond merely contingent, instrumental attachments, it takes daily life down to a deeper level than some passing parade of personal moods and feelings. By its nature, institutional thinking tends to cultivate belonging and a common life.

To be sure, works of modern fiction routinely portray rebellion against all institutions as courageous adventures of liberation. The promise is perfect freedom. But that promise is an illusion. The truth—to be found in any reliable work of nonfiction (whether history, biography, or current events)—is that a life devoid of institutional attachments becomes a perfect hell of self-destructive excesses. At the center of such real-life accounts is the ultimate excess, the overweening self-life. Without authority for freedom to play against, the liberation adventure extinguishes itself in existential meaninglessness. When you really look at the facts of everyday life, the "adventure" of total self-liberation turns out to be a self-destructive trajectory. That is the real story line about the egoists in our modern celebrity culture. Throughout our tabloids and Internet blogs, the sub-texts are usually appealing to an inward, unarticulated moral outlook. Our popular culture loves its celebrity heroes, but it loves even more the sight of their crumbling self-made pedestals. That is a backhanded way of affirming that there really are pedestals of merit on which to stand, even though the humans atop may be rather wobbly.

There are good, commonsense reasons why an anti-institutionalist perspective does not work in real life (which is a world quite different from the thought-palaces of many tenured intellectuals). However much we might pretend otherwise, we humans are not complete enough to complete ourselves. We are not rich enough that we can do without institutional attachments and intergenerational kisses. We simply do not have the fullness of resources that would be required. If nothing is important but self-fulfillment, there is nothing of substance available to help us do the filling.

Thinking institutionally offers us a more excellent way of being in the world. It demarcates a middle zone of liberating constraints. To the one side is the lone cultural wanderer facing a bewildering array of choices. Because they are self-validating, they are choices without any larger substantial meaning. Whatever peace and meaning is to be found must come from internally generated expressions of the Self and resistance to all external threats to one's autonomous self-determination. To the other side of the institutionalist's zone is the yearning for unity and a pooling of particularities into something whole. It is the totalizing vision that answers to the cultural wanderer's lostness. The promise is an "I" capable of knowing itself only because it is absorbed into a monistic "we."

The institutionalist middle zone yields a more realistic view of life. Human beings find meaning as they live in the tension between the universal and the particular, between what has been given and what is not yet fulfilled. This middle zone does not claim to provide ultimate meaning, because thinking institutionally is not a religion or comprehensive secular ideology. It is a place for finding proximate, human-scale meanings. Such meaning emerges through engagement in the historical tasks and obligations that lie at hand for each one of us. These are the mundane but rewarding tasks and obligations embodied in institutions that involve family, work, education, local community, religious congregation, citizenship, and—to return to where we started—sports.

And increasingly we are realizing that the same institutional way of thinking should apply to whatever piece of geography we happen to occupy. Our piece of earth and proximate surroundings are another kind of middle zone, a localization that participates in a larger world environment. Through force of physical circumstance, we moderns are having to learn what it means to faithfully receive, to infuse with value and thoughtfully pass on to others our earth home. Again, events rather than philosophical arguments are mainly teaching us the lesson. The material world is not simply an ensemble of objects for our use; it is something that makes a claim on us and our sense of stewardship. We lead implicated lives. "The environment" is only the most visible object in a larger world of human relationships that is suffering and quite possibly decomposing for want of institutional thinking.

So what should you and I do? Perhaps one day someone will produce a self-help book or twelve-step program for those who want to improve their lives by thinking institutionally. That is not on offer here. It makes no sense to exhort people to be good or think institutionally until they have a better understanding of what that good thing is. Many people do have a sense of the matter even if they cannot verbalize it very well. That is why from time to time I have appealed to a common-sense understanding that we seem to share about such things as sportsmanship, marriage, law, and the first day of school. We should take this as a sign of hope for the future. The "appreciative viewpoint" I have called thinking institutionally forms a deep stratum in our human makeup. It does not need to be invented by some social philosopher or political leader. It needs to be recovered and articulated. Hence this book's rationale.

Thinking institutionally is really not that difficult to understand. We more or less know it when we see it. It is simply very difficult to live out. This way of thinking and being in the world is hard work. The reasons for this have been discussed in the last chapter. So, awaiting publication of the next self-help book and twelve-step program, what is a person to do? Like all the advice we have heard regarding a healthful diet and exercise program, the practical answer is as straightforward to state as it is difficult to carry out.

Moral realism understands that the grand movements of history, from life to death and everything in between, are played out in the particular acts of individuals. Those acts, influenced as they must be by all sorts of larger contextual factors, remain choices that we as moral agents have the freedom to make or not make. They are not the automatic result of blind, deterministic necessity. Institutionalists have an essentially hopeful view, believing in a better future. That is why they try to use the materials of the past to invest in that future.

At the same time, thinking and acting institutionally does not come easily for us, especially in light of the modern dangers and obstacles it faces. Institutional thinking is learned. And it is learned, or not learned, in the home, the schools, the marketplace, and the political forum. It cannot be learned if it is not taught, and most teaching occurs through example. Doesn't that tell us something we should do?

A recent multiyear study has tried to understand how people in various domains of employment come to do "good work." What the researchers mean by this term is not only a high "job" performance rating but work that reflects a humane, responsible, and consistent quality of moral behavior. Good work is what our earlier discussion subdivided into the concepts of profession, office, and stewardship. Anyone who has read this far will not be surprised by the researchers' findings. What fosters such good work is, first, a strong sense of moral commitment to larger purposes that one brings to the job; second, the professional ethic exemplified by those individuals providing a person with his or her early job training; and finally, the "lineages" of worthy models from the past with whom one identifies in working toward the future.[3] In short, a person learns to think institutionally by being around and identifying with people who model and reinforce one's appreciation for institutional values. This produces a gradual, perhaps only half-conscious shaping of character.

For anyone left wondering what to do, the most practical advice on this matter is also the most ancient. A person learns to think and act institutionally by doing it. In that sense it is like an "art." It is not a matter of learning philosophical arguments. It is a matter of doing it in order to learn more deeply about what one is doing. Aristotle put it this way: "The virtues we get by first exercising them, as also happens in the case of the arts. For the things we have to learn before we can do them, we learn by doing them, for example, men become builders by building and lyre players by playing the lyre. So too we become just by doing just acts, temperate by doing temperate acts, brave by doing brave acts."[4]

This sounds rather abstract, but it is actually quite practical. In fact, to acquire a way of thinking, institutional or otherwise, is probably the most practical thing a person ever does. So, for example, in today's atmosphere of cynical distrust, there is at least one thing you and I can realistically do to raise the level of healthy trust in society. It may be the only thing we can do. That is to strive to be trustworthy. The same advice applies to all the other aspects of being institutionally minded that we have discussed. By carrying out the actions that follow from thinking institutionally, we enhance a culture of institutional values. Therefore, while our modern culture does shape us, we also shape our culture by the ways of thinking and being that we choose to embrace. The *habitus* that makes up our daily lives marks the point of contact where other people are touched by and may be brought to consider institutional values. Our example is much more important than any theoretical model or book on the subject.

There is no golden age of institutional values to return to, but neither need we remain stuck where we are in our modern impasse. To repeat, living in a world of nothing but institutional thinking would be a monstrosity. But to live in a world in which institutional thinking is absent, or so heavily discounted as to fade into insignificance, would be an even greater monstrosity. The evidence lying all around us is hardly ambiguous. Our current danger is not too much but too little institutional thinking. The modern mind has lost its equilibrium with regard to institutions. The Enlightenment taught us to think for ourselves, and the Romantic countermovement taught us to express ourselves. The rise of bureaucratized mass industrial society showed that we had to protect the Self, and the development of our consumer society has assured all of these Selves that we have a right to have things our way, and quickly so. The cultural upheaval of the 1960s insisted on having it both ways: on the one hand to be dismissive of institutions as mere formalities that we could remake at will and on the other to thoroughly condemn institutions as oppressive power structures of the Establishment.

It is surely ironic that as long-term commitments, institutional and otherwise, are fading from the modern consciousness, we humans are now on the verge of living longer than our kind has ever dared hope to live. But buried in that statement is something more important than the possibility of long life. We are the creature that hopes. We are not just an animal that "wants" for the next meal or mating or escape from a predator. In our nature we pass beyond the bounds of wanting to a realm of things greater than we have experienced and yet have the capacity to yearn for. Of course, we can tell ourselves that it might be wishful thinking. But even in telling ourselves that, we are affirming some minimal faith in the possibility of a larger, hopeful truth of things. We have at least enough faith to doubt and ask questions. And the answers we yearn for are not a sweet brew of lies.

Thanks to medical technology we, our children, and grandchildren are now being promised a vast expansion in the human life span (unless we willfully eat, drink and/or smoke ourselves to an early death). The old 70 and 80 may become the new 150 or 200. Is that good or bad news? I think we will discover that long life is not what we really hoped for. Mere longevity will not take away the sadness of a self-life that offers no larger meaning and yet cannot help yearning for such meaning. Our longer time span will then appear as simply the lengthening of autumnal shadows felt by the aging medievalist:

> Time of mourning and of temptation,
> Age of tears, of envy and of torment,
> Time of languor and of damnation,
> Age that brings us to the end,

Time full of horror which does all things foolishly,
Lying age, full of pride and envy,
Time without honor and without true judgment,
Age of sadness which shortens life.[5]

Should it occur, humankind will probably survive any eventual triumph of anti-institutionalism, whatever our life span. Our species has a very clever, small-mammal quality to it—a quickness, adaptability, and subtlety of maneuver that will probably help us avoid extinction.

The larger question, of course, is whether we will survive as something more than mere survivors, that is, as something in the image of what it is to be fully human. As individuals and as a society, we need not lose our bearings on that subject. There is available to us a valid, though incomplete, vision of that fuller image. It is the reflection caught in our deep-seated human capacity to think and act institutionally. We would do well to take that capacity more seriously—to learn about it, appreciate it, teach it, and act on it.

"Does the road wind uphill all the way?" Yes, to the very end. But that is no reason to lose heart. The way up can also be the way out, toward something better.

NOTES

Chapter 1

1. W. J. Morgan, "The Logical Incompatibility Thesis and Rules: A Reconsideration of Formalism as an Account of Games," in W. J. Morgan and K. Meier eds., *Philosophic Inquiry in Sport* (Champaign, IL: Human Kinetics, 1995), 61. For a more thorough discussion, see F. D'Agostino, "The Ethos of Games," *Journal of the Philosophy of Sport* 8 (1981): 7–18.

2. See, for example, Heather Sheridan, "Conceptualizing 'Fair Play': A Review of the Literature," *European Physical Education Review* 9, no. 2 (2003): 163–184; Craig Clifford and Randolph M. Feezell, *Coaching for Character* (Champaign, IL: Human Kinetics, 1997); William J. Morgan, Klaus V. Meier, and Angela J. Schneider eds., *Ethics in Sports* (Champaign, IL: Human Kinetics, 2001).

3. This speech is at www.baseballhalloffame.org/news/2005/sandberg_speech.doc, accessed 8/1/06.

4. Richard Sennett, *The Culture of the New Capitalism* (New Haven, CT: Yale University Press, 2005).

5. For some prominent presidential examples prior to George W. Bush, see Eric Alterman, *When Presidents Lie: A History of Official Deception and Its Consequences* (New York: Penguin, 2005).

6. See Hearings of the U.S. House of Representatives Oversight and Government Reform Committee in April 2007, summarized in *Military News,* http://www.marinecorpstimes.com.

7. A thorough account of Lawrence Summers's presidency at Harvard has yet to be written, but the broader context for that failure is discussed in Harry R. Lewis, *Excellence without a Soul* (New York: Pub-

lic Affairs, 2006). The story of Harvard's Institute for International Development is recounted in David McClintick, "How Harvard Lost Russia," *Institutional Investor* (January 2006).

8. David L. Kirp, *Shakespeare, Einstein, and the Bottom Line: The Marketing of Higher Education* (Cambridge, MA: Harvard University Press, 2005); Larry Cuban, *The Blackboard and the Bottom Line: Why Schools Can't Be Businesses* (Cambridge, MA: Harvard University Press, 2004).

9. William A. Sullivan, *Work and Integrity: The Crisis and Promise of Professionalism in America* (San Francisco: Jossey-Bass, 2005), and on the legal profession in particular, Sol M. Linowitz, *The Betrayed Profession: Lawyering at the End of the Twentieth Century* (New York: Scribner's, 1999).

10. Jean Bethke-Elshtain, quoted in Eric Miller, "Alone in the Academy," *First Things* (February 2004): 32.

11. Accounts of the performance of these three women, who were selected as "persons of the year," can be found in *Time* 160, no. 2 (December 30, 2002–January 6, 2003): 30–60. The quotation from the Rowley memo to FBI director Robert Mueller is from page 37.

12. Quoted in Seymour M. Hersh, "Annals of National Security: The General's Report," *New Yorker*, June 25, 2007, 69. On Alberto Mora, see Jane Mayer, "Annals of the Pentagon: The Memo," *New Yorker*, February 27, 2006, 32–41, and more generally, Jack Goldsmith, *The Terror Presidency: Law and Judgment inside the Bush Administration* (New York: Norton, 2007).

13. From the last scene of F. Scott Fitzgerald, *The Great Gatsby*, edited by Matthew J. Bruccoli (New York: Cambridge University Press, 1991), 141.

14. Jonathan Haidt, *The Happiness Hypothesis: Finding Modern Truth in Ancient Wisdom* (New York: Basic Books, 2005). The rapidly expanding field of "positive psychology" is providing evidence-based studies of happiness, something quite different from the faddish "self-esteem" movement. Tal Ben-Shahar, *Happier: Learn the Secrets to Daily Joy and Lasting Fulfillment* (New York: McGraw Hill, 2007).

Chapter 2

1. Benjamin Wittes, *Confirmation Wars: Preserving Independent Courts in Angry Times* (Lanham, MD: Rowman and Littlefield, 2006). While the public's approval of the Court's performance has remained stable and high, confidence in the institution itself has fallen since 2000.

2. The Annenberg Democracy Project, *A Republic Divided* (New York: Oxford University Press, 2007), 59–63 and 216–217. In this instance, the Annenberg Institutions of Democracy survey in January 2005 asked, "Generally speaking, how much do you trust the federal government in Washington to operate in the best interests of the American people?" The four responses available were a "great deal," a "fair amount," "not too much," and "not at all."

3. Seymour Martin Lipset and William Schneider, *The Confidence Gap: Business, Labor, and Government in the Public Mind,* rev. ed. (Baltimore: Johns Hopkins University Press, 1987). Until recently in the United States, courts have retained a high and stable level of trust, while confidence in the military has grown since relevant data began to be gathered in the early 1970s.

4. World Economic Forum, "Full Survey: Trust in Governments, Corporations and Global Institutions Continues to Decline," *GlobeScan Report on Issues and Reputation* (Washington, DC: GlobeScan, December 2005). A comprehensive summary of the evidence among the advanced industrial nations, focused mainly on political trust, is in Russell J. Dalton, *Democratic Challenges, Democratic Choices: The Erosion of Political Support in Advanced Industrial Democracies* (New York: Oxford University Press, 2004). For a more benign view of a transformation rather than erosion of legitimacy, see Achim Hurrelmann et al., "Is There a Legitimation Crisis of the Nation-State?" in Stephan Leibfried and Michael Zurns, eds., *Transformations of the State?* (New York: Cambridge University Press, 2005), 119–137.

5. Vivian Hart, *Distrust and Democracy* (Cambridge: Cambridge University Press, 1978).

6. A. Tversky and D. Kahneman, "Advances in Prospect Theory: Cumulative Representation under Uncertainty," *Journal of Risk and Uncertainty* 5 (1992): 7–323.

7. A good primer on the subject is Kenneth R. Gray, Larry A. Frieder, and George W. Clark, *Corporate Scandals: The Many Faces of Greed* (St. Paul, MN: Paragon House, 2005).

8. Eric M. Uslaner, "Producing and Consuming Trust," *Political Science Quarterly* 115, no. 4 (2000–2001): 569–590.

9. John S. Glaser, *The United Way Scandal: An Insider's Account of What Went Wrong and Why* (New York: John Wiley and Sons, 1993).

10. Margaret Gibelman and Seldon R. Gelman, "Very Public Scandals: Nongovernmental Organizations in Trouble," *Voluntas, International Journal of Voluntary and Nonprofit Organizations* 12, no. 1 (March 2001): 49–66.

11. Paul Light, *The Continued Crisis in Charitable Confidence* (Washington, DC: Brookings Institution, 2004). A subsequent poll by Harris Interactive released in the summer of 2006 found that only 10 percent of Americans strongly believe charities are "honest and ethical" in their use of donated funds, while almost 30 percent believe that nonprofits have "pretty seriously gotten off in the wrong direction."

12. Sissela Bok, *Lying: Moral Choice in Public and Private Life* (New York: Pantheon, 1978).

13. These contrasting interpretations are presented in Jack Citrin and Donald Philip Green, "Presidential Leadership and the Resurgence of Trust in Government," *British Journal of Political Science* 16 (1986): 431–453; and John T. Williams, "Systemic Influences on Political Trust: The Importance of Perceived Institutional Performance," *Political Methodology* 11 (1985): 125–142.

14. Suzanne Garment, *Scandal: The Crisis of Mistrust in American Politics* (New York: Random House, 1991). Lippman's classic work on the subject is *Public Opinion*, first published in 1922.

15. Among early crossovers was young congressmember Richard Nixon's use of public relations experts in his 1950 California Senate race and the America Medical Association's post–World War II Champaign against national health insurance ("Socialized Medicine"). Stanley Kelly, *Professional Public Relations and Political Power* (Baltimore: Johns Hopkins University Press, 1966). The early story of the PR industry is told by its founding father in Edward L. Bernays, *Public Relations* (Norman: University of Oklahoma Press, 1952).

16. Roper, speaking in 1949, is quoted to this effect in Bernays, *Public Relations*, page 151.

17. Niklas Luhmann, *Trust and Power* (New York: John Wiley, 1979).

18. Daniel Yankelovich, *New Rules: Searching for Fulfillment in a World Turned Upside Down* (New York: Random House, 1981), 16. More detailed discussions of this impact of the 1960s are in Alan Ehrenhalt, *The Lost City: Discovering the Forgotten Virtues of Community in the Chicago of the 1950s* (New York: Basic Books, 1995); Alan Wolfe, *One Nation, After All* (New York: Viking, 1998); Wayne Baker, *America's Crisis of Values: Reality and Perception* (Princeton, NJ: Princeton University Press, 2005), 55–60; and "The Sixties and the Origins of 'Postmodern' America," in Robert Griffith and Paula Baker, eds., *Major Problems in American History since 1945: Documents and Essays* (New York: Houghton Mifflin, 2007), 270–278.

19. Jean-Jacques Rousseau, *Emile: Or on Education* (Basic Books, 1979 [1762]), 43.

20. C. Wright Mills, *The Power Elite* (New York: Oxford University Press, 1956).

21. *On the Usefulness of Believing,* section 26, para. 1743.

22. Tina Cassidy, *Birth: The Surprising History of How We Are Born* (New York: Atlantic Monthly Press, 2006).

23. Charles Wagner, *The Simple Life* (New York: McClure, Phillips, 1903), 39–40. Interesting experimental evidence to this effect is reported in Harold Garfinkel, "A Conception of, and Experiments with, 'Trust' as a Condition of Stable Concerted Actions," in O. J. Harvey ed., *Motivation and Social Interaction* (New York: Ronald Press, 1963), 189.

24. The quotation can be found on Brewster's grave marker in Grove Street Cemetery, New Haven, Connecticut.

25. Roger Lundin, *From Nature to Experience: The American Search for Cultural Authority* (Lanham, MD: Rowman and Littlefield, 2005), quoting Dorothy Sayers, page 201.

Chapter 3

1. In addition to sources cited below in note 41, helpful reviews are in Robert E. Goodin, ed., *The Theory of Institutional Design* (Cambridge: Cambridge University Press, 1996), 1–22; and J. E. Lane and S. Ersson, *The New Institutional Politics* (London: Routledge, 2000).

2. In some cases I have changed phrasing to make the definitions more concise, but I hope not to have misrepresented any author's original meaning. The sources are:

    1. R. Matthews, "The Economics of Institutions and the Sources of Growth," *Economic Journal* 96 (1986): 905.

    2. R. A. W. Rhodes, "Old Institutionalisms," in Rhodes, Sarah A. Binder, and Bert A. Rockman, eds., *The Oxford Handbook of Political Institutions* (New York: Oxford University Press, 2006), 92.

    3. Theodore Lowi, *The End of Liberalism: The Second Republic of the United States* (New York: W. W. Norton, 1969).

    4. Margaret Levi, *Of Rule and Revenue* (Berkeley: University of California Press, 1988), 3, 16.

    5. Talcott Parsons, *The Social System* (New York: Free Press, 1951), 39; "Prolegomena to a Theory of Social Institutions," *American Sociological Review* 55, no. 3 (1990): 324.

6. S. N. Eisenstadt, "Social Institutions: The Concept," in *International Encyclopedia of the Social Sciences* (New York: Macmillan, 1968), 409.

7. Thorstein Veblen, "The Limitations of Marginal Utility," in *The Place of Science in Modern Civilization* (New York: Russell and Russell, 1961), 239.

8. Philip Selznick, *The Moral Commonwealth: Social Theory and the Promise of Community* (Berkeley: University of California Press, 1992), 233.

9. Walton Hamilton, "Institution," in *Encyclopaedia of the Social Sciences* (New York: Macmillan, 1962), 84.

10. Jack Knight and James Johnson, "The Priority of Democracy," *American Political Science Review* 101, no. 1 (February 2007): 47.

11. Stephen Skowronek, *Building a New American State: The Expansion of National Administrative Capacities, 1877–1920* (New York: Cambridge University Press, 1982), 1–19.

12. Elizabeth Sanders, "Historical Institutionalism," in Rhodes et al., eds., *The Oxford Handbook of Political Institutions*, 39–44.

13. Kenneth A. Shepsle, "Studying Institutions: Some Lessons from the Rational Choice Approach," *Journal of Theoretical Politics* 1, no. 2 (1989): 135.

14. Douglass C. North, *Institutions, Institutional Change, and Economic Performance* (Cambridge: Cambridge University Press, 1990), 3.

15. William H. Riker, "Implications from the Disequilibrium of Majority Rule for the Study of Institutions," *American Political Science Review* 74, no. 2 (June 1980): 432.

16. Andrew Schotter, quoted in Ole Winckler Andersen and Kirsten Bregn, "New Institutional Economics: What Does It Have to Offer?" *Review of Political Economy* 4, no. 4 (1992): 487.

17. Robert Calvert, "Rational Actors, Equilibrium and Social Institutions," in Jack Knight and Itai Sened, eds., *Explaining Social Institutions* (Ann Arbor: University of Michigan Press, 1995), 73–74.

18. John W. Meyer and Brian Rowan, "Institutionalized Organizations: Formal Structure as Myth and Ceremony," in Walter W. Powell and Paul J. DiMaggio, eds., *The New Institutionalism in Organizational Analysis* (Chicago: University of Chicago Press, 1991), 44.

19. Ronald Jepperson, "Institutions, Institutional Effects, and Institutionalism," in Powell and DiMaggio, eds., *The New Institutionalism in Organizational Analysis,* 149.

20. Roger Friedland and Robert R. Alford, "Bringing Society Back In: Symbols, Practices, and Institutional Contradictions," in Powell and DiMaggio, eds., *The New Institutionalism in Organizational Analysis,* 249.

21. Mary Douglas, *How Institutions Think* (Syracuse, NY: Syracuse University Press, 1986), 48.

3. John Rawls, "Two Concepts of Rules," *Philosophical Review* 64 (1955): 3–32. The multiple meanings of the term *rule* are surveyed in J. S. Ganz, *Rules: A Systematic Study* (The Hague: Mouton, 1971); and S. B. Shimanoff, *Communication Rules: Theory and Research* (Beverly Hills, CA: Sage, 1980).

4. Paul Edwards, ed., *The Encyclopedia of Philosophy* (New York: Macmillan, 1967), 314.

5. March and Olson 1984, 741; William H. Riker, "Implications from the Disequilibrium of Majority Rule for the Study of Institutions," *American Journal of Political Science* 74 (1980): 432–447.

6. Roughly speaking, this was Aristotle's approach in investigating the meaning of terms such as "constitution" or "friendship," and Wittgenstein's view of the definition of "games." Ludwig Wittgenstein, *Philosophical Investigations* 32e (para. 67), G. E. M. Anscombe, trans., 3rd ed. (Malden, MA: Blackwell, 1958).

7. Peter Hall and Rosemary Taylor, in "Political Science and the Three New Institutionalisms," *Political Studies* 44, no. 4 (1996): 936–953, distinguish between historical, rational choice, and sociological approaches, while broader surveys are provided in Guy Peters, *Institutional Theory in Political Science: The New Institutionalism* (London: Pinter, 1999); and Vivien Lowndes, "The Institutional Approach," in David Marsh and Gerry Stoker, eds., *Theory and Methods in Political Science* (Houndmills, UK: Palgrave, 2002). The incommensurable nature of the various schools is described in Robert Adcock, Mark Bevir, and Shannon Stimson, "Historicizing the New Institutionalisms," in Robert Adcock, Mark Bevir, and Shannon Stimson, eds., *Modern Political Science: Anglo-American Exchanges since 1880* (Princeton, NJ: Princeton University Press, 2006).

8. *The History of Government from the Earliest Times,* vol. 1 (New York: Oxford University Press, 1997), 1–4.

9. *The Moral Commonwealth: Social Theory and the Promise of Community* (Berkeley: University of California Press, 1992), 5–9.

10. Kathleen Thelen, *How Institutions Evolve* (New York: Cambridge University Press, 2004), 10–12.

11. Douglass C. North, *Institutions, Institutional Change, and Economic Performance* (New York: Cambridge University Press, 1990), 13–17.

12. Richard W. Scott, *Institutions and Organizations* (Thousand Oaks, CA: Sage, 2001), 18–21.

13. This example was first used by Joseph Schumpeter. He pointed out there was no more paradox in protecting intellectual property to promote creativity than in saying that motorcars are traveling faster than they otherwise would because they are provided with brakes. Joseph A. Schumpeter, *Capitalism, Socialism and Democracy*, 5th ed. (London: Allen and Unwin, 1976), 88.

14. Robert H. Bates, Avner Greif, Margaret Levi, Jean-Laurent Rosenthal, and Barry R. Weingast, *Analytic Narratives* (Princeton: Princeton University Press, 1998). This and other areas of overlap are discussed in Kathleen Thelen, "Historical Institutionalism in Comparative Politics," *Annual Review of Political Science* 2 (June 1999): 369–404; and Kenneth A. Shepsle, "Rational Choice Institutionalism," in R. A. W. Rhodes, Sarah A. Binder, and Bert A. Rockman, eds., *The Oxford Handbook of Political Institutions* (New York: Oxford University Press, 2006).

15. Jacob S. Hacker, "Privatizing Risk without Privatizing the Welfare State: The Hidden Politics of Social Policy Retrenchment in the United States," *American Political Science Review* 98, no. 2 (2004): 243–260.

16. Ruth Berins Collier and David Collier, *Shaping the Political Arena* (Princeton, NJ: Princeton University Press, 1991).

17. Karen Orren and Stephen Skowronek, *The Search for American Political Development* (Cambridge: Cambridge University Press, 2004); Wolfgang Streeck and Kathleen Thelen, eds., *Beyond Continuity: Institutional Change in Advanced Political Economies* (Oxford: Oxford University Press, 2005).

18. Jean Blondel, "About Institutions, Mainly, but Not Exclusively, Political," in Rhodes, Binder, and Rockman, *The Oxford Handbook of Political Institutions*. Leading examples are Theda Skocpol, *States and Social Revolutions: A Comparative Analysis of France, Russia and China* (Cambridge: Cambridge University Press, 1979); and Steven Skowronek, *Building a New American State: The Expansion of National Administrative Capacities, 1877–1920* (New York: Cambridge University Press, 1982).

19. These differing, but not contradictory, views are presented in John E. Chubb and Terry M. Moe, *Politics, Markets, and America's Schools* (Washington, DC: Brookings Institution, 1990); John W. Meyer, "The Effects of Education as an Institution," *American Journal of Sociology* 83, no. 1 (July 1977): 55–77; and John W. Meyer and Brian Rowan, "Institutionalized Organizations: Formal Structure as Myth and Ceremony," *American Journal of Sociology* 83, no. 2 (1977): 340–363.

20. Lon L. Fuller, *The Morality of Law* (New Haven, CT: Yale University Press, 1969), chap. 1.

21. The terms are taken, respectively, from John Rawls, "Two Concepts of Rules"; and Roger Friedland and Robert R. Alford, "Bringing Society Back In: Symbols, Practices, and Institutional Contradictions," in Walter W. Powell and Paul J. DiMaggio, eds., *The New Institutionalism in Organizational Analysis* (Chicago: University of Chicago Press, 1991); Robert E. Goodin, "Institutions and Their Design," in Robert E. Goodin, ed., *The Theory of Institutional Design* (Cambridge: Cambridge University Press, 1996).

22. Paul R. Milgrom, Douglass C. North, and Barry R. Weingast, "The Role of Institutions in the Revival of Trade: The Law Merchant, Private Judges, and the Champagne Fairs," *Economics and Politics* 2, no. 1 (1990): 1–23.

23. Douglass C. North and Barry R. Weingast, "Constitutions and Commitment: The Evolution of Institutions Governing Public Choice in Seventeenth-Century England," *Journal of Economic History* 49 (1989): 803–832.

24. Karl W. Deutsch, *The Nerves of Government: Models of Political Communication and Control* (New York: Free Press, 1963), 111.

25. Douglass North, 1993 Nobel Lecture, http://nobelprize .org/nobel_prizes/economics/laureates/1993/north-lecture.html, accessed August 7, 2007.

26. Douglas Southall Freeman, *George Washington: A Biography,* vol. 4 (New York: Charles Scribner's Sons, 1951).

27. From the standpoint of his personal self-interest, Washington clearly understood that the rational course would be to decline the job. As he said to a fellow delegate from Virginia, "Remember, Mr. Henry, what I now tell you: from the day I enter upon the command of the American armies, I date my fall, and the ruin of my reputation." Freeman, *George Washington,* vol. 3, page following page 436.

28. Freeman, *George Washington,* vol. 4, page 338.

Chapter 4

1. Clifford Geertz, "Ethos, World View, and the Analysis of Sacred Symbols," in *The Interpretation of Cultures, Selected Essays* (New York: Basic Books, 1973), chap. 5.

2. Daniel C. Dennett, *The Intentional Stance* (Cambridge: Massachusetts Institute of Technology Press, 1987); Sir Geoffrey Vickers, *The Art of Judgment* (New York: Basic Books, 1965).

3. H. L. A. Hart, *The Concept of Law* (Oxford: Clarendon Press, 1961), 59–60, 86–88, and 95–96. A kindred perspective is Clifford Geertz's interpretive approach in *Local Knowledge* (New York: Basic Books, 1983).

4. The following account in indebted to I. C. Jarvie, *The Republic of Science: The Emergence of Popper's Social View of Science 1935–1945;* as well as to its original source in Karl Popper, *The Logic of Scientific Discovery* (London: Hutchinson, 1962). A critical survey of related views is in John Wettersten, "Essay Review of The Republic of Science," *Philosophy of Science* 73 (January 2006): 108–121.

5. Thomas S. Kuhn, *The Structure of Scientific Revolutions* (Chicago: University of Chicago Press, 1970).

6. Michael Polanyi, *Personal Knowledge: Towards a Post-Critical Philosophy* (Chicago: University of Chicago Press, 1958).

7. William H. Whyte, Jr., *The Organization Man* (New York: Simon and Schuster, 1956), 3.

8. Quoted in *Time* double issue (December 30, 2002/January 6, 2003): 37.

9. *Virgil: The Aeneid,* Robert Fagles, trans. (New York: Viking, 2006).

10. David Stewart, "The Hermeneutics of Suspicion," *Journal of Literature and Theology* 3 (1989): 6–307.

11. Peter A. Facione, *Critical Thinking: A Statement of Expert Consensus for Purposes of Educational Assessment and Instruction* (Millbrae, CA: California Academic Press, 1990).

12. Peter A. Facione, "Critical Thinking: What It Is and Why It Counts," *Insight Assessment* (2007): 11.

13. Facione, *Critical Thinking,* 1.

14. As reported in *Harvard Magazine* (July–August 2007): 68.

15. Pier Paolo Vergerio (1370–1444), "The Character and Studies Befitting a Free-Born Youth," in Craig W. Kallendorf ed., *Humanist Educational Treatises* (Cambridge, MA: Harvard University Press, 2002), 29.

16. Available at http://www.president.harvard.edu/news/inauguration.

17. Alfred North Whitehead, *An Introduction to Mathematics* (New York: Henry Holt, 1911), 61.

18. "The Perpetuation of Our Political Institutions," address before the Young Men's Lyceum of Springfield, Illinois, January 27, 1838, in *Abraham Lincoln: Speeches and Writings 1832–1858* (New York: Library of America, 1989), 28–36.

19. Roger Kimball, *The Rape of the Masters: How Political Correctness Sabotages Art* (San Francisco: Encounter Books, 2004).

20. The French seem to have a knack for expressing this deep contrast between sadness and exhilaration in relation to one's self-creation or rootedness. Compare, for example, Gilles Deleuze, *Pure Immanence: Essays on a Life* (New York: Zone Books, 2001), with Simone Weil, *The Need for Roots* (New York: G. P. Putnam's Sons, 1952).

21. Philip Selznick, *Leadership in Administration* (Berkeley: University of California Press, 1957), 17.

22. Charles Taylor, *Sources of the Self* (Cambridge, MA: Harvard University Press, 1989), 4.

23. A fuller treatment would show that there is more complexity than I am suggesting here. The intellectual intricacies involved in considering how values arise in the processes of self-formation and self-transcendence are the subject of Hans Joas's book *The Genesis of Values* (Chicago: University of Chicago Press, 2000).

24. Lon L. Fuller, *The Morality of Law* (New Haven, CT: Yale University Press, 1969), 39–94.

25. This is the point at which Hart's "internal point of view" on the law is constructively deepened by John Finnis in his *Natural Law and Natural Rights* (Oxford: Clarendon Press, 1980). A useful brief overview of the legal positions is contained in Robert P. George, "What Is Law? A Century of Arguments," *First Things* 112 (April 2001): 23–29.

26. Paul R. Amato and Stacy J. Rogers, "Do Attitudes toward Divorce Affect Marital Quality?" *Journal of Family Issues* 20, no. 1 (January 1999): 69–86.

27. John Donne, *The Annunciation and Passion*, in C. A. Patrides, ed., *The Complete English Poems of John Donne* (London: Dent and Sons, 1985), 452.

28. Richard Labunski, *James Madison and the Struggle for the Bill of Rights* (New York: Oxford University Press, 2006). A valuable review is by Gordon S. Wood, "Without Him, No Bill of Rights," *New York Review of Books* 53, no. 19 (November 30, 2006).

29. Given the delays in transatlantic communication, Madison received Jefferson's letter of September 9, 1789, only a few days before he responded to it on February 4, 1790. The texts of both letters can be found at the Annals of American History website, http://america.eb.com/america. Helpful discussions of the exchange are in Adrienne Koch, *Jefferson and Madison: The Great Collaboration* (New York: Knopf, 1950), 62–96; Merrill Peterson, "Thomas Jefferson's 'Sovereignty of the Living Generation,'" *Virginia Quarterly Review* 52 (1976): 437–444; and David N. Mayer, *The Constitutional Thought of Thomas Jefferson* (Charlottesville: University Press of Virginia, 1994), 302–308.

30. Letter to John Wayles Eppes, 1813 (ME 13:270). See also letters to Samuel Kercheval, July 12, 1816 (ME 15:42); Thomas Earle, 1823 (ME 15:470); Major John Cartwright, June 5, 1824.

31. Interestingly enough, Jefferson seems to have gotten part of his wish for France. Although the legal Napoleonic Code remained all but frozen in time, France went through seventeen constitutions from 1789 to the present, an average of roughly one every thirteen years.

32. Jefferson's view helps one understand how his Monticello estate, over which he labored so intensely for his own pleasure, ended up on the auction block a mere five years after his death. It was a tale of shortsighted, irresponsible mismanagement. See Alan Pell Crawford, *Twilight at Monticello: The Final Years of Thomas Jefferson* (New York: Random House, 2008). Madison, too, ended his years in financial distress. But the different reasons compared with Jefferson's are revealing. Madison spent significant sums paying off the debts of his stepson from Dolley Madison's first marriage. More important, his Piedmont estate could not compete with the production of fertile lands to the west using the Mississippi River for transit. For his entire career Madison had promoted free transit of the Mississippi as a boon to future generations. Madison did believe in intergeneration obligations, even if it threatened his financial security.

33. A good job of sorting through Madison's complex and at times contradictory statements on states' rights and the national union is in Kevin Raeder Gutzman, "From Interposition to Nullification: Peripheries and Center in the Thought of James Madison," *Essays in History* 36 (1994).

34. Harry V. Jaffa, *Crisis of the House Divided: An Interpretation of the Issues in the Lincoln-Douglas Debates* (Chicago: University of Chicago Press, 1959), 228; Garry Wills, *Lincoln at Gettysburg: The Words That Remade America* (New York: Simon and Schuster, 1992).

35. Bernard Bailyn, *To Begin the World Anew* (New York: Knopf, 2003), chap. 4. The literature is obviously immense, but one does well

to begin with Gordon S. Wood, *The Creation of the American Republic, 1776–1787* (Chapel Hill: University of North Carolina Press, 1969); and Jack N. Rakove, *The Beginnings of National Politics: An Interpretive History of the Continental Congress* (Baltimore: Johns Hopkins University Press, 1979).

36. Here I borrow and modify language from Harvey C. Mansfield, Jr., *America's Constitutional Soul* (Baltimore: Johns Hopkins University Press, 1991), 15. My characterizations of this generation are by no means intended to deny its intense and often vicious partisanship. See Stanley Elkins and Eric McKitrick, *The Age of Federalism* (New York: Oxford University Press, 1993).

37. Chantal Delsol, *Icarus Fallen: The Search for Meaning in an Uncertain World* (Wilmington, DE: ISI Books, 2003).

Chapter 5

1. Erving Goffman, *The Presentation of Self in Everyday Life* (New York: Doubleday Anchor, 1959); Niklas Luhmann, *Trust and Power* (New York: Wiley and Sons, 1979). Luhmann argues that system trust ultimately depends on personal trust, but others dispute the necessary connection. Eric M. Uslaner, *The Moral Foundations of Trust* (New York: Cambridge University Press, 2002).

2. Recognition of this problem has prompted the Carnegie Foundation's Preparation for the Professions Program. See William A. Sullivan, *Work and Integrity: The Crisis and Promise of Professionalism in America* (San Francisco: Jossey-Bass, 2005). Interestingly enough, the first of the foundation's special studies concerns the education of clergy in the United States. See Charles R. Foster et al., eds., *Educating Clergy: Teaching Practices and Pastoral Imagination* (New York: Wiley and Sons, 2006).

3. David A. Bella, "Engineering and Erosion of Trust," *Journal of Professional Issues in Engineering* 113 (1987): 117–129.

4. Talcott Parsons, "Research with Human Subjects and the 'Professional Complex,'" in Paul Freund, ed., *Experimentation with Human Subjects* (New York: George Braziller, 1970).

5. Bernard Barber, *Informed Consent in Medical Therapy and Research* (New Brunswick, NJ: Rutgers University Press, 1980).

6. George Annas, *Some Choice: Law, Medicine, and the Market* (New York: Oxford University Press, 1998); and Nancy Tomes, "Patients or Health-Care Consumers? Why the History of Contested Terms Matters," in Rosemary A. Stevens, Charles E. Rosenberg, and Lawton R.

Burns, eds., *History and Health Policy in the United States* (New Brunswick, NJ: Rutgers University Press, 2006).

7. This is represented in the work of Dennis F. Thompson, *Restoring Responsibility: Ethics in Government, Business, and Healthcare* (New York: Cambridge University Press, 2004). For the legal profession, see John T. Noonan, Jr., and Richard W. Painter, *Professional and Personal Responsibilities of the Practicing Lawyer* (New York: Foundation Press, 1997); and for a would-be public administration professional, see John A. Rohr, *Public Service, Ethics, and Constitutional Practice* (Lawrence: University Press of Kansas, 1998), and John J. Gargan, "The Public Administration Community and the Search for Professionalism," in Jack Rabin, W. Bartley Hildreth, and Gerald J. Miller, eds., *Handbook of Public Administration,* 3rd ed. (Boca Raton, FL: CRC Press, 2006), 1126–1204.

8. For the sake of brevity I am merging the notions of duty and obligation. The two can reasonably be differentiated as regards the requirements of office and the requirements of contractual promises. See R. B. Brandt, "The Concepts of Obligation and Duty," *Mind* 73, no. 1 (July 1964): 374–393.

9. Thomas E. Mann and Norman J. Ornstein, *The Broken Branch: How Congress Is Failing America and How to Get It Back on Track* (New York: Oxford University Press, 2006).

10. Alexander M. Bickel, *The Supreme Court and the Idea of Progress* (New York: Harper and Row, 1970); John T. Noonan, Jr., and Kenneth I. Winston, eds., *The Responsible Judge: Readings in Judicial Ethics* (New York: Praeger, 1993).

11. M. T. Griffin and E. M. Atkins, eds., *Cicero, On Duties* (New York: Cambridge University Press, 1991), 3.

12. Christopher Lasch, *Haven in a Heartless World: The Family Besieged* (New York: Basic Books, 1977); Vigen Guroian, "Family Offices," *Touchstone* 18, no. 6 (July–August 2005): 36–41.

13. While the term "role" has come to be used more carelessly, the original understanding in social science was similar to the traditional concept of office. As Ralph Linton put it, a status is a collection of rights and duties, and "a role represents the dynamic aspect of a status. . . . [I]t puts the rights and duties which constitute the status into effect." Ralph Linton, *The Study of Man: An Introduction* (New York: D. Appleton-Century, 1936), 113.

14. This discussion of stewardship is only weakly related to the rational choice school's principal–agent theory, which assumes a strictly contractual relationship and an inherent conflict in goals between the

principal and the agent. Terry Moe, "The New Economics of Organization," *American Journal of Political Science* 28 (1984): 756.

15. Despite some resemblances, this fiduciary trust is obviously not the same kind of asymmetry of power and dependence discussed earlier with the concept of profession. See Bernard Barber, *The Logic and Limits of Trust* (New Brunswick, NJ: Rutgers University Press, 1983).

16. What we are referring to here is in Latin *procuratio,* the supervision of another man's business interests, usually translated as "management." This is different from *tutela,* or the guardianship of a person unable to manage his or her own affairs.

17. James Madison, letter of March 27, 1792, quoted in G. Hunt, ed., *The Writings of Madison,* vol. 6 (New York: G. P. Putnam, 1900–1910), 101–103.

18. Adolph A. Berle and Gardner C. Means, *The Modern Corporation and Private Property* (New York: Macmillan, 1932); Dennis F. Thompson, "The Possibility of Administrative Ethics," *Public Administration Review* 45 (September–October 1985): 555–561; Henry D. Kass, "Stewardship as a Fundamental Element in Images of Public Administration," in Henry D. Kass and Bayard L. Catron, eds., *Images and Identities in Public Administration* (Newbury Park, CA: Sage, 1990).

19. The quotation is from Chief Justice Cardoza in *Meinhard v. Salmon,* in the New York Supreme Court, 249 N.Y. 458, 164 N.E. 545 (1928). Cardoza went on: "A managing co-adventurer appropriating the benefit of such lease without warning to his partner might fairly expect to be reproached with conduct that was underhanded, or lacking, to say the least, in reasonable candor, if the partner were to surprise him in the act of signing the new instrument. Conduct subject to that reproach does not receive from equity a healing benediction."

20. Thus a book like David Swensen's *Unconventional Success* (New York: Free Press, 2005) is valuable not least because it is pitched at a popular level that can allow ordinary citizens to see what is actually at work in the world of investment "stewardship."

21. This is not to deny that in the business and financial fields there are all sorts professional associations as well as credentialing and licensing operations that seek to promote adherence to codes of conduct. The problem is that they so frequently appear irrelevant in practice. Dean Neu, "New Stock Issues and the Institutional Production of Trust," *Accounting, Organizations and Society* 16 (1991): 185–200.

22. Terence R. Mitchell and William G. Scott, "Leadership Failures, the Distrusting Public, and Prospects of the Administrative State," *Public Administration Review* (November–December 1987): 449–450.

23. Lynne G. Zucker, "Production of Trust: Institutional Sources of Economic Structure, 1840–1920," *Research in Organizational Behavior* 8 (1986): 52–111. The more recent history is described in Susan P. Shapiro, "The Social Control of Impersonal Trust," *American Journal of Sociology* 93 (1987): 623–658.

24. In public administration circles, the argument over achieving administrators' responsibility through inner standards or external controls has continued since the "Friedrich-Finer debate" of 1940. See Laurence E. Lynn, Jr., "Public Management," in B. Guy Peters and Jon Pierre, eds., *Concise Handbook of Public Administration* (Newbury Park, CA: Sage, 2007). Recent analyses roughly favorable to the stewardship view are in John A. Rohr, *To Run a Constitution: The Legitimacy of the Administrative State* (Lawrence: University Press of Kansas, 1986); and Gary L. Wamsley, "The Agency Perspective: Public Administrators as Agential Leaders," in Gary L. Wamsley et al., eds., *Refounding Public Administration* (Newbury Park, CA: Sage, 1990).

25. Jerome B. Karabel, *The Chosen: The Hidden History of Admission and Exclusion at Harvard, Yale, and Princeton* (New York: Houghton Mifflin, 2006).

26. Michael Thomas, Richard Ellis, and Aaron Wildavsky, *Cultural Theory* (Boulder, CO: Westview Press, 1990).

27. Philip Selznick, *The Moral Commonwealth: Social Theory and the Promise of Community* (Berkeley: University of California Press, 1992), 243.

28. Elizabeth Fox-Genovese and Eugene D. Genovese, *The Mind of the Master Class: History and Faith in the Southern Slaveholders' Worldview* (New York: Cambridge University Press, 2005).

29. That is the language on an award given to one Mary Livingston, an archivist for the federal government who, by doing the duties of her office, prevented a fraudulent donation of vice presidential papers that would have netted her boss, President Nixon, a $450,000 tax break. Her obituary is in the *Washington Post,* March 25, 2007, C7.

30. A good place to begin is with Karen DeYoung, *Soldier: The Life of Colin Powell* (New York: Knopf, 2006).

31. Frederic M. Litto, "Addison's Cato in the Colonies," *William and Mary Quarterly,* 3d ser., 23 (1966): 431–449.

32. Eliot's actual lines take us deeper; they can be accessed online at http://www.americanpoems.com/poets/tseliot/1076.

33. Former Connecticut governor and convicted felon John Rowland, quoted in the *Washington Post,* June 17, 2007, D7.

34. The older books on this subject remain well worth reading. Karl Polanyi, *The Great Transformation: The Political and Economic Origins of Our Time* (Boston: Beacon Press, 1980); Peter Laslett, *The World We Have Lost: Further Explored* (New York: Scribner's, 1984). More than economic exploitation, it was the crushing of the human spirit and social community that drove the young Karl Marx's hatred of the market economy and capitalism. T. B. Bottomore, *Karl Marx: Early Writings* (London: C. A. Watts, 1963).

35. Alexis de Tocqueville, *Democracy in America*, J. P. Mayer and Max Lerner, eds., George Lawrence, trans. (New York: Harper and Row, 1966), 591.

36. John Clark Ridpath, *Ridpath's History of the World*, vol. 9 (Cincinnati, OH: Jones Brothers Publishing, 1901), 488.

37. Eva Illouz, *Consuming the Romantic Utopia: Love and the Cultural Contradictions of Capitalism* (Berkeley: University of California Press, 1997).

38. Richard Sennett, *The Culture of the New Capitalism* (New Haven, CT: Yale University Press, 2005).

39. Tocqueville, *Democracy in America*, 520, 557.

40. *The Memoirs of John Q. Adams*, vol. 8 (Philadelphia: Lippincott and Co., 1875), 519.

41. Tocqueville, *Democracy in America*, 590.

42. Ibid., 393–394.

43. Robert Bellah et al., *Habits of the Heart* (Berkeley: University of California Press, 1985).

44. Charles Taylor, *Sources of the Self* (Cambridge, MA: Harvard University Press, 1989), 503.

45. Helpful summaries of the scholarly debates are in John Robertson, *The Case for the Enlightenment: Scotland and Naples, 1680–1760* (New York: Cambridge University Press, 2007); and Keith Michael Baker and Peter Hanns Reill, eds., *What's Left of Enlightenment? A Postmodern Question* (Palo Alto, CA: Stanford University Press, 2001).

46. Peter Gay, *The Enlightenment: An Interpretation* (New York: W. W. Norton, 1977), 130.

47. E. J. Hundert, *The Enlightenment's Fable: Bernard Mandeville and the Discovery of Society* (New York: Cambridge University Press, 2005).

48. Gay, *The Enlightenment*, 358–380.

49. Reinhold Niebuhr, *The Nature and Destiny of Man*, vol. 2 (New York: Charles Scribner's Sons, 1964), 148–169.

50. Taylor, *Sources of the Self*, 508.

51. Quoted in Edward Mozejko, *Between Anxiety and Hope: The Poetry and Writing of Czeslaw Milosz* (Alberta: University of Alberta Press, 1988), 107.

Chapter 6

1. Andrew Keen, *The Cult of the Amateur: How Today's Internet Is Killing Our Culture* (New York: Random House, 2007).

2. John Kelley, *The Great Mortality* (New York: HarperCollins, 2004).

3. This project being conducted by Howard Gardner at Harvard University is accessible at http://pzweb.harvard.edu/pis/hg.htm.

4. *Nicomachean Ethics,* Book II, chap. 1.

5. Eustache Deschamps, quoted in Johan Huizinga, *The Autumn of the Middle Ages* (Chicago: University of Chicago Press, 1996), 32.

APPENDIX
SELECTED WORKS
OF HUGH HECLO

Modern Social Politics: From Relief to Income Maintenance (Yale University Press 1974)

A Government of Strangers: Executive Politics in Washington (Brookings Institution 1977)

The Illusion of Presidential Government, coedited with Lester Salamon (Westview Press 1981)

Policy and Politics in Sweden, with Henrick Madsen (Temple University Press 1987)

The Private Government of Public Money: Community and Policy Inside British Politics, with Aaron Wildavsky, 3rd ed. (Macmillan 1990)

Comparative Public Policy: The Politics of Social Choice in Europe and America, with Arnold Heidenheimer and Carolyn Adams, 3rd ed. (St. Martin's 1990)

The Government We Deserve, with C. Eugene Steurele, Edward M. Gramlich, and Demetra Smith Nightingale (Urban Institute Press 1998)

Religion Reenters the Public Square: Faith and Policy in America, coedited with Wilfred M. McClay (John Hopkins University Press 2003)

Christianity and American Democracy (Harvard University Press 2007)

INDEX

Abbey, Edward, 158
Abu Ghraib Prison, 6, 8
Accountability, 148–149
Adams, John Quincy, 169
Aeneas, 91
American Revolution, 72–75, 114, 125
Aristotle, 5, 41, 192–193
Aromony, William, 23
Augustine, St., 40

Baby Boom generation, 17, 28
Bernard of Clairvaux, 137
Bill of Rights (U.S.), 112–113, 114, 117, 123, 124, 144
Black death, 188
Blair, Jason, 5
Bogart, Humphrey, 25
Brewster, Kingman, 42
Brookings Institution, 24
Buber, Martin, 51
Bureaucratization: contemporary, 37, 65, 90, 135, 162; historical, 63, 148–149, 164–167, 178–181, 193
Business organizations, 15–17, 145, 147, 163–164, 167–168, 179

Cardozo, Benjamin, 146, 211n19
Cato, 160
Christian church, 136–137
Christie's Auction House, 16
Cicero, 137, 140, 141
Cobain, Kurt, 108
Cognitive school, 55–56, 63
Congress (U.S.), 12, 72–73, 112, 114, 125, 140
Constitution, U.S., 12, 112–113, 122–123, 124, 126
Consumer culture, 7, 166–167, 180, 194
Contractual relations, 57, 106, 123, 171
Cooper, Cynthia, 8
Covenantal relations, 106, 123
Critical thinking, 91–97, 107, 175
Cynicism, 13, 25, 30–31, 158, 183, 193

Dante, 43, 137
Debt, 6, 98, 116, 119–120
Declaration of Independence, 123
Democracy, 34–35, 168–172, 175
Descartes, Rene, 171
Dewey, John, 34
Dickens, Charles, 110

Diderot, Denis, 175
Display effect, 27, 30
Distrust: of institutions, culture-based, 32–42; 11–14, 43, 95, 135, 183, 187; performance-based, 15–32
Donne, John, 109
Douglas, Mary, 151
Dunlap, Al, 5
Durkheim, Emile, 53
Duty, 77–78, 91, 102–103, 136–141, 157, 181, 188, 210n8

Ebbers, Bernie, 5
Eliot, T. S., 162
England, 69–70
Enlightenment, the, 174, 175, 177, 179, 180, 193
Enron, 5, 8, 15

Federal Bureau of Investigation (FBI), 8, 90
Federal government, 12, 22–23, 154
Fiduciary relationships, 41, 143, 146–147, 188
Foucault, Michel, 108
French Revolution, 107, 111–112, 118, 175
Functionalism, 55

Gates, Horatio, 77
Geertz, Clifford, 81
Geneva Convention, 8
Glorious Revolution of 1688, 70
Goethe, 99, 156
Golden Rule, 34, 35, 37, 39
Great Gatsby, 9
Gregory VII, 137

Habitus, 81–82, 183, 193
Happiness, 9, 39, 83, 84, 190
Harvard University, 6, 94, 95, 96, 150
Healy, Bernadine, 24
Hepburn, Katharine, 25

Higher education. *See* Universities
Hiroshima, bombing of, 188
Historical-institutionalist school, 54, 62
Hitler, Adolph, 79, 149–150, 151, 156–157
Hoover, J. Edgar, 90
Hume, David, 137
Hurricane Katrina, 12

Individualism, 36, 106–108, 192–193
Institute for International Development, 6
Institutions: definitions of, 35, 38, 46–52; examples of, 4, 12–13, 55, 89, 129, 190–191; good versus bad, 132, 149–156, 177, 183, 187; purposes of, 64, 77–78, 87–88, 90, 91, 101–105, 107, 130–132, 134, 139–140, 152–154, 177, 192
Instrumental rationality, 63, 66, 174, 177, 179, 181, 186
Internet, 28, 186, 189
Iraq War, 6, 12

Jefferson, Thomas, 111–123, 145, 208n32
Jesus, 142, 145
Joplin, Janice, 108
Judges, 140

Kant, Immanuel, 103, 174
Kelley, Jack, 5
King's power problem, 70, 72, 76, 124
Klein, Joe, 5

Lampedusa, Guiseppe di, 99
La Rochefoucauld, 65
Law, 104, 118–121, 134, 143, 154, 183, 191. *See also* Rule of law
Law Merchant system, 68–69, 72, 74, 124
Lay, Ken, 5

Leadership, 25–26, 30, 31–32, 127, 162, 182
Leary, Timothy, 108
Lee, Charles, 76
Liberal education, 94–95, 173
Lincoln, Abraham, 98, 100, 123, 155, 182
Lippman, Walter, 27, 28
Livingston, Mary, 212n29
Llewellyn, Karl, 46
Louis XVI, 111, 113
Love Canal, 16
Lynch, Jessica, 6

Madison, James, 111–123, 126, 144, 145, 160, 182, 208n32
Mafia, 149
Majoritarianism, 121, 172
Marriage, 84, 105–106, 129, 134, 191
Marx, Karl, 164
Mason, George, 159
Meinhard v. Salmon, 146
Merrill Lynch, 16, 26
Mill, John Stuart, 33
Mills, C. Wright, 38
Milosz, Czeslaw, 184
Modernity, 11, 33, 36, 45, 100–101, 103, 108, 122, 157, 174, 179–181, 193
Mora, Alberto, 8
Moral agency, 79, 82–83, 88, 92, 93–94, 102, 192
Morality of aspiration, 65, 76, 77, 104–105, 132, 158, 182, 187
Mother Theresa, 151

New institutionalism, 47
Nixon, Richard, 200n15, 212n29
Nongovernmental organizations (NGOs), 23–24
North, Douglas, 66, 71

Office, 25, 136–142, 162, 170, 172, 177, 192

Organizational analysis, 63–65, 90, 133, 162

Parliament, British, 69
Path dependency, 54
Peace Corps, 132
Pelikan, Jaroslav, 99
Pilgrim's Progress, 182
Ponzi, Charles, 26, 28
Popular culture, 7, 9, 182, 187, 189
Postmodernism. *See* Modernity
Powell, Colin, 159
Precedent, 109–110
Presentism, 188
Presidency, 12, 140
Professions, 8, 12, 41, 129, 133–135, 136, 139, 142, 162, 177, 192; training for, 7, 133, 135, 147
Property, 143–144
Public administration, 145, 147, 183, 212n24
Public relations, 27–30, 41
Putnam, Israel, 76

Rather, Dan, 5
Rational choice school, 54–55, 58–59, 63, 66–70, 71, 73, 123–124
Rawls, John, 47–50
Red Cross, 23
Respect in depth, 4, 66, 89, 102, 133, 147, 182, 186
Ridpath, John, 166
Robertson, Donald, 160
Romanticism, 178–179, 180, 181, 193
Roper, Elmer, 28
Rousseau, Jean Jacques, 36, 42, 118, 177
Rowley, Coleen, 8, 90
Rule of law, 24, 104–105, 124, 158. *See also* Law

Sandberg, Ryan, 3–4, 8, 102, 159, 187–188
Scale effect, 26–27, 30
Schools, public, 34, 64–65, 82, 92, 96, 134–136, 191
Science, natural, 85–88, 130, 176
Science, social, 14, 46, 82–83, 106, 141, 150–153, 161, 176, 210n13; schools in, 52–56, 66, 78, 84
Scientific method, 86–87, 92, 104
Securities and Exchange Commission (SEC), 16
Shakespeare, William, 100, 137–138
Shaw, George Bernard, 34
Sisyphus, 182
Sixties, 35, 135, 194
Skepticism, 13
Slavery, 149, 155–156
Smith, Adam, 164
Social systems school, 53–54
Sotheby's Auction House, 16
Sports, 1–4, 5–6, 99, 101, 154, 190, 191
Statist school, 53, 63
Stendhal, Henri, 159
Stewardship, 110, 142–149, 156, 162, 170, 178, 191, 192, 210–211n14, 211n20
Stuart monarchy, 69–70
Substantive rationality, 65, 187

Summers, Lawrence, 197n7
Supreme Court, 12

Taguba, Antonio, 8
Taubman, Alfred, 16
Taylor, Charles, 102, 173–174
Tillman, Pat, 6
Tocqueville, Alexis de, 165, 168–172
Transaction costs, 67, 71, 124

United Way, 23
Universities, 6–7, 61, 78, 82, 92, 96–97, 100, 135, 158, 173, 182
Usufruct, 110–111, 115, 117, 122, 145
Utopianism, 107–108, 128, 178

Vietnam War, 6
Virgil, 91

Ward, Artemas, 76
Washington, George, 72–77, 124, 159, 182, 205n26
Watkins, Sherron, 8
Weber, Max, 63, 165
Whyte, William, 90
Witherspoon, John, 160
WorldCom, 5, 8, 15

Yankelovich, Daniel, 35

ABOUT THE AUTHOR

Hugh Heclo is Clarence J. Robinson Professor of Public Affairs at George Mason University, a former Professor of Government at Harvard University, and prior to that a Senior Fellow at the Brookings Institution. His latest book, *Christianity and American Democracy,* was published by Harvard University Press in 2007.